Migration and Ethnicity
in
Northeast India

Migration and Ethnicity in Northeast India

Editors
M. Amarjeet Singh
H. Shukhdeba Sharma

Maulana Abul Kalam Azad Institute of Asian Studies, Kolkata

SHIPRA

Rs. 900; US$ 36

ISBN: 978-93-88691-36-9

First Published in India in 2020

Migration and Ethnicity in Northeast India

Published by:
SHIPRA PUBLICATIONS
LG 18-19, Pankaj Central Market
I.P. Ext., Patparganj, Delhi 110092, India
Tel.: +91 11 2223 5152/6152, 9650028065
E-mail: info@shiprapublication.com
www.shiprapublication.com

Foreword

I'm delighted to learn that a Seminar Proceeding on "Migration & Ethnicity in Northeast India" is being brought out by MAKAIAS. A two-day seminar on the theme was organized by Maulana Abul Kalam Azad Institute of Asian Studies (MAKAIAS), Kolkata in collaboration with Centre for North East Studies & Policy Research (CNESPR) Jamia Millia Islamia (JMI), New Delhi and Indira Gandhi National Tribal University-Regional Campus Manipur (IGNTURCM) at Imphal, Manipur on 23-24 February 2018. The articles in this volume attempt to establish broad historical outlines by connecting the problem of migration and ethnicity as existed in the past to the problem existing today. Case based analyses of continuities & discontinuities based on the challenges and opportunities bear upon multiple perspectives of North East Region & the migration problem. A wide array of papers focusing on different aspects of the problem of migration makes the volume academically rich and helps understanding the complex problem of migration. I hope the volume will continue to interest the scholars and researchers in a comparative study of migration problem in North East Region.

There are three models of migration discussed: "Classical Model", "Colonial Model" and the "Guest Worker Model" that existed since 1945 across the world. The perspectives of these models are extended to issues of Migration to North East India in finding solutions to the present crisis. Colonial migration provides the historical link to movement of people inside the country; incidentally the internal migration also continues during postcolonial period because of the nature of our polity along with people constantly coming in and moving out from a particular territorial space for other reasons as well. What remained critical are the politics of identity and the fear of being outnumbered by outsiders in one's own land. Therefore, we cannot view migration only as movement of people from outside the national border or from within, it has a serious repercussion on resources, land use and political representation. Illegal migration is a huge issue and politically a very sensitive one at that. Although resolution to the problem may not be readily available but understanding of the problem then seeking a positive solution is more important than other concerns. It is in this context some of the papers in the volume have demonstrated acute awareness of the problem with insights and have tried to offer some solution to the complex problem. The problem has given rise to various forces that use it to whip up emotions and create social and political unrest.

This volume although attempts to address problems associated with migration & ethnicity of North East India, it also recognizes the need for new methodologies for the study in order to come up with creative solutions. In this sense, the book presents an opportunity not only for reflection on and review of existing ideas but also providing the means that better reflect the reality of the region. Policy makers and scholars having interest in the region, I'm sure, will find this volume useful.

Sujit K. Ghosh
Chairman
Maulana Abul Kalam Azad Institute of Asian Studies
Kolakata

29.07.2019

Preface

In recent years, we can observe that migration is taking place in a greater number than ever before, with almost all countries rapidly becoming either the sender or receiver of migrants. However, there are numerous restrictive policies adopted by different countries to control migration. Several countries are worried by migration of their high-skilled workers into other countries, but encourage migration of the unskilled workforce. Similarly, several other countries have adopted restrictive policies on whom they would like to either admit or exclude. Despite these restrictions, many people continue to resort to irregular means to enter the country of their choice.

In case of India's Northeast, the advent of colonial rule brought significant transformations in the migration patterns of the region. The migration of labour to the region was motivated by colonial exploration of the region's rich resources, which considerably changed the demography of the region. In due course of time, the unabated immigration became the main reason for the insecurity of the indigenous inhabitants. Their insecurity has further been worsened since wholesale and retail trade in the region is largely controlled by the immigrant communities. But, the liberalisation of the Indian economy has brought a large number of young people from all over the country for work towards major cities. Among them are many youth from the region who are engaged in different service professions.

In order to discuss these issues, a two-day national-level seminar entitled *Migration and Ethnicity in Northeast India* was organised by Maulana Abul Kalam Azad Institute of Asian Studies (MAKAIAS), Kolkata, in collaboration with Centre for North East Studies and Policy Research (CNESPR), Jamia Millia Islamia (JMI), New Delhi and Indira Gandhi National Tribal University-Regional Campus Manipur (IGNTU-RCM) at IGNTU-RCM, Makhan on 23-24 February 2018. It was attended by a large number of scholars from various parts of the country.

At JMI, we are very grateful to Prof. Talat Ahmad, the then Vice-Chancellor; Mr. A.P. Siddiqui, the Registrar; Prof. Simi Malhotra, Director, CNESPR; Mr. K. Kokho, Assistant Professor, CNESPR; Ms. Anamika Deb Roy, Assistant Professor, CNESPR; and Prof. R.S. Thakur, the then Director of IGNTU-RCM for their guidance and support.

We are also extremely grateful to Dr. G. Maheshwari, Director, MAKAIAS, Kolkata, and Prof. V.K. Srivastava, the former Director of MAKAIAS, for their support in holding the seminar in Manipur and the subsequent efforts to publish the present book.

We have not selected all the papers presented during the seminar for the present book. All the selected papers have undergone extensive internal and external referring over a period of several months. We are indebted to Dr. Komol Singha, Dr. Rimi Tadu, Ms. Dolly Limbu, Mr. Bikas Chetri, Mr. Tarunkumar Sharma, Mr. Himat Tampakmayum and Mr. Alan Mustofa for taking their valuable time for providing us with valuable comments.

M. Amarjeet Singh
H. Shukhdeba Sharma

Contents

Introduction

M. Amarjeet Singh and *Dolly Limbu*

In a restricted sense, migration can be understood as 'permanent or semi-permanent change of usual residence', across some types of demarcated space or administrative boundary (*see* Wood, 1994) into new ones due to a number of push-and-pull factors. To put it simply, the movement within a country may be understood as the 'internal migration', while the movement from a country to another as the 'international migration'. However, studies at large have proven that internal migration is more difficult to assess, given the nature of people's movement. The parameters of internal migration fail to approximate as in, how far a person has to move or stay in the destination place to be considered as a migrant. The key approach in such migration is to usually recorded if a person has moved from an administrative unit to another. However, this definition leaves out relocation within the unit. Nonetheless, there is no universally accepted answer, although official censuses adopted one-year threshold. Such official definition will leave out seasonal migration.

Although international migration has garnered both scholarly and public attention, internal migration has relatively been less explored. In fact, the latter actually deserves a proper channel for research and extensive study as it is far more significant in relation to the number of people who are involved in the migration process. The contribution of internal migrant labour towards the economy of affected countries is either underplayed or ignored by many governments and "escape the responsibility of providing them with adequate living conditions, minimum wages and freedom from exploitation and harassment" (Deshingkar and Grimm, 2004; 6).

The effects of migration can be seen in demographic, economic and political aspects in the places of origin, transit and destination. It allows millions of people to escape from poverty, religious and political oppression.

It has been observed that individual migrants "reap gain in the form of higher incomes, better access to education and health and improved prospects for their children" (United Nations Development Programme, 2009; 2). Therefore, the migrants have better chances of experiencing upward mobility than the non-migrants (Lopreato and Hazelrigg, 2015; 408). In short, migration has increasingly become a global phenomenon in which the livelihoods of a large number of people and their families have been directly affected.

Migration is a universal phenomenon and has transpired and shaped human history. In today's global world, it is an inevitable experience and the era of rapidly increasing migration is usually referred to as the age of migration (King et al, 2010). It is generally acknowledged that migration is a global phenomenon (Hirst et al, 2009; 29). But in reality, it is growing steadily rather than exponentially (*see* UNDP, 2009). An increasing number of countries are now "either country of origin, transit or destination for migrants, and increasingly are all three simultaneously" (Berne Initiative, 2004; 2-8). Thus, the division between the origin (sending), and destination (receiving) countries is no longer relevant because most countries have become the countries of origin, transit and destination (Duvell, 2010; 289-310). Reflecting on the contemporary transformation of migration, the International Organisation for Migration (IOM), the inter-governmental organisation, had remarked:

> None of the roughly 190 sovereign nations in the international system is now beyond the reach of migration circuit. Indeed, they are all either country of origin, transit or destination for migrants, and increasingly are all three simultaneously. Migration circuits span the globe like a spider's web, with complex ramifications and countless intersections. The current world map of migration is, therefore, multipolar (International Organisation for Migration, 2013; 4).

Consequently, we have witnessed a further diversification of the already diverse ethnicities of many countries such as Canada, the USA, Britain, France and Australia (*see* Vertovec, 2010).

Globalisation and neoliberal paths have a direct bearing upon urbanisation and migration in India too. More than three-quarters of the population in developed countries live in urban areas in comparison to that, less than half of the population in developing countries inhabit the urban region. Rapid population growth is expected in the urban areas of less developed regions, averaging 2.3 per cent per year during this period, and almost all of the world's population growth is expected to take place in the urban areas of less developed countries (Ministry of Health and Family Welfare, 2009; 6). Another prominent feature of urbanisation in developing countries is the top-heavy urban hierarchy. In fact, most of the large cities in the world are now located in developing countries. At the same time, the rapid population growth has brought a host of problems, including crowding, environment degradation, slums, disparities in living conditions and access to services and increasing vulnerability to diseases and poor health (Ministry of Health and Family Welfare, 2009; 6).

Globally, about three million people are supposedly migrating to cities every week. Migrants constitute over a third of the population in Sydney, London and New York, and for more than half in Brussels and Dubai (International Organization for Migration, 2015; 1). Urbanisation and manufacturing are mainly responsible for short- and long-term migration in Southeast and East Asia (Deshingkar and Grimm, 2004; 7). International migrants in Singapore, Kuala Lumpur, Hong Kong and Bangkok can be categories into (i) professional and managerial expatriates: Mostly from India and the Philippines, as well as from Europe, North America, Japan, Republic of Korea, Australia and New Zealand; (ii) international students; and (iii) low-skilled migrant workers: They constitute the largest group who mainly come from other Asian countries (International Organisation for Migration, 2015; 54). Migrants are often challenged with legal (in the case of international migrants), cultural and social barriers in obtaining public services in the destination places due to (i) linguistic barriers, (ii) legal and administrative barriers, (iii) reduced access to social networks, (iv) reduced knowledge of the local environmental and social context, (v) inadequacy of skills for urban labour market, and (vi) lack of representation, discrimination and xenophobia (International Organization for Migration 2015, 81-82).

Delhi, the national capital of India, is one of the fastest growing cities in the world. It has undergone a swift change from being predominantly rural to predominantly urban (Government of Delhi, 2015; 1). Its population has been growing at a rapid pace since Independence. Historically, the partition of India resulted in a great incursion of refugees into this city. In addition, the attainment of Independence and the resultant need to develop the national capital created a huge demand for manpower and therefore, there was a tremendous influx of immigrants into the city especially from nearby states (*see* Government of India, 1987; 14-16).

In short, the following pattern has been observed in migration. It has accelerated its flow and movement in recent decades. It has also found to be diversified in most countries which receive different types of migrants in contrast with earlier times when particular forms of immigration, such as labour immigration or refugees were predominant. There is greater globalisation of migration involving many countries/places as senders and recipients. Additionally, we have seen increasing feminisation of migration in recent decades (King et al, 2010), including the migration from Northeast India to other cities of the country.

Migration has traditionally been dominated and engineered by men. However, the trend is fast changing in recent decades with more and more young women migrating to earn their livelihoods, not just accompanying their spouses. This has been possible due to "a greater demand for female labour in certain services and industries and also because of growing social acceptance of women's economic independence and mobility" (Deshingkar and Grimm, 2004; 15). Available data indicate that women's migration is 'very high' in South America and Southeast Asia. Majority of the female migrants in East and Southeast Asia are young and unmarried; and the concentration of these groups is greatest in the megacities (Deshingkar and Grimm, 2004; 15). Although female migration has increased remarkably in South Asia in recent decades, it is still not on the scale of South America and Southeast Asia. Nonetheless, the cultural barriers that prevented them from stepping out of their homes are gradually breaking down.

Remittances by migrants have significantly contributed to the well being and consumerism among the migrant families. For example, remittances from the Gulf to Kerala have been "converted into status through conspicuous consumption, large houses and automobiles" (Rao, 1986; 26).

Nonetheless, migration has always been restricted, and the government from around the world had adopted policies determining the type and direction of migration in the nineteenth century (Fahrmeir et al, 2003; 3). Labour-sending countries considered migration of their high-skilled workers into another country as brain drain but encouraged the unskilled ones to do so because the latter could bring remittances and new skills. In fact, these countries preferred immigration of high-skilled workers. Thus, the reception of immigrants in the host countries could be: low receptivity, permitted (but not actively encouraged), and privileged reception (Portes and Böröcz, 1989; 606-630).

Although, migration is a self-sustaining diffusion process (Massey et al, 1997) which is exclusively dependent on social networks, and in fact aids in generating such furthering social networks. Such "networks are the sets of interpersonal ties that connect migrants, former migrants and non-migrants in sending and destination areas through ties of kinship, friendship and shared community origins" (Massey, 1999; 48). Such networks provide short-term adaptive assistance, such as housing, even money, information and emotional support to the migrants. "Once migration connections have been established, the presence of relatives, friends and others from the same community of origin may form strong incentives to choose a particular destination" (Massey et al, 1993).

Furthermore, when a significant number of migrants have been recruited into certain occupations, the latter is viewed to be socially undesirable for the native people. In such a situation, the natives will be socially conditioned to not employ themselves in such sectors. Migration, therefore, can change the social definitions of work as native jobs and immigrant jobs, and the latter is defined as stigmatising for the native people. The stigma of immigrant jobs comes from the presence of migrants, not from the characteristics of the occupation (Bohning, 1974; 155-163). In such a situation, the main assets the immigrants bring to their destination places are cheap labour, willingness to work harder and loyalty to their employers. Thus, migration performs a dual function: (i) for capital, it is a source of more abundant and less expensive labour; and (ii) for the immigrants, it is a means of survival, and a vehicle for social integration and economic mobility (Portes and Böröcz, 1989; 606-630).

It has also been noted that increasingly several prospective migrants who cannot migrate legally, resort to unauthorised means such as illegal entry and overstaying a legally obtained visa or permit. This form of migration occurs outside the ascendency of authorised means. But there is a difficulty in categorising "the typology of such migration or even to know what terminology to use, due to the complexity of the issue and diverse contexts in which it occurs" (Brennan, 1984; 409). Illegal migration has been a concern since countries define the extent of their territorial sovereignties and national space. Thus, migration controls became an instrument of demarcation of boundaries and of enforcement of its crucial means. At the same time, it is rare to come across any country which is unaffected by unauthorised migration. Viewing from a narrower perspective, unauthorised migration challenges the self-contained autonomy of the nation-states (Morris, 1997) because recognition of the sovereignty of nation-state means recognition of the inviolability of its borders and its final authority over what goes on within the borders. Thus, unauthorised border crossing is the violation of sovereignty. But unauthorised border crossing has become a fundamental aspect of global migration (Duvell, 2005; 16). However, there is no population census on illegal migration, the estimates are usually influenced by the methodology utilised and by the agenda of those reporting (International Organization for Migration, 2009; 207), as in India. In reference to the adult illegal migrants, Sonia McKay *et al* (2011) argues that they are in the 'healthiest' phase of their lives as they are more willing and accepting of poor living and working conditions. This may be attributed to the fact that they treat such exploitative situations and setting as a temporary challenge, but such enforced acceptance has largely been due to the absence of alternatives. This model of subservient labour is witnessed predominately, although not exclusively, in global cities (Sonia et al, 2011).

Global migration since 1945 can be broadly divided into three types. Firstly, the *Classic Model* applies to Canada, the United States, Australia, etc. which have developed as the nation of immigrants. In this case, immigration was encouraged to a considerable extent. Secondly, the *Colonial Model* was pursued by France and the United Kingdom, which favoured immigrants from the former colonies. In fact, a large number of immigrants to the United Kingdom in the years following the Second World War were mainly from the Commonwealth countries. Thirdly, the *Guest Worker Model* was employed by Germany, Switzerland and Belgium in which immigrants were admitted on a temporary basis, often in order to fulfil demands of the labour market, but did not receive citizenship rights even after long period of settlement (for more information, please *see* Russell King et al, 2010).

An individual's decision to migrate is influenced by a range of factors that are beyond his/her realisation. Some scholars convincingly argue that the push-pull theory of migration places undue importance on the role of the individual and ignores the wider social contexts that may affect their choices. They view migration as an interaction, at one level, between events and circumstances in the wider world and at the other, the individual situation of the migrant. They are increasingly looking at global migration patterns as 'systems' which are produced through interaction between the macro-level and micro-level processes. Macro-level factors are the overarching issues such as the political situation, laws and regulations about migration or changes in the international economy. Micro-level factors, on the other hand, are concerned with the resources, knowledge and understandings that the migrant populations themselves possess (*see* Russell King et al, 2010).

Migration is also an interesting topic among social science disciplines despite the theoretical divides based on disciplines and political positions (Castles, 2008; 7), and is often studied within a nationalist framework (Schendel, 2005; 2-3). Thus, much of the literature is prescriptively attempting to persuade the readers to support one or another solution to the problem (Portes, 1978).

In the official, media and academic discourses in India, the terms such as Northeast India, North-East, Northeast Region, NE and NER are used interchangeably. These terms which began to be used explicitly in the 1960s, were further bolstered with the setting up of the North Eastern Council, a public funded planning agency, in 1972; and subsequently in 2004 with the setting up of the Ministry of the Development of North Eastern Region, the ministry aimed to facilitate the planning, execution and monitoring of infrastructure projects of this region. Hence, this region is the only part of the country having an exclusive ministry allocated with sufficient funds to reduce the economic gap with the rest of the country. However, their efficacy remains a matter of debate, and further examination is needed in the said field. This is beyond the scope of this book.

In terms of its topography, around three-fourths of the land, the North Eastern region is hilly which is characterised by difficulties in physical connectivity. Owing to the peripheral nature of the region, factors such as underdevelopment, isolation and difficulties in physical connectivity have restricted the region from the purview of the mainstream media and national dialogue. The remoteness coupled with pitiable physical connectivity and underdevelopment has led to the alienation of a significant portion of its inhabitants due to their lack of integration into the mainstream of the national life.

The creation of new border can prove to be either peaceful or violent. The partition of India into India and Pakistan came at the cost of the millions of lives. The partition not only resulted in communal rioting and trauma in both the countries, it consequently displaced and uprooted people permanently from their homes. A stark contrast to this was the separation of Burma from British India in 1937 which was marked by a peaceful transition of power. Before the partition, the region comprising of Bengal, Assam and Arakan formed a trade corridor. It was however severely affected by the shifting and redrawing of the border which in turn affected the flow of goods and people. The partition took the region's economy backwards by a quarter of a century, and catching up with rest of the county was a mammoth task (Ministry of Development of North Eastern Region and North Eastern Council, 2008; 1).

For a long time, the plain areas of the region were exposed to a strong socio-cultural influence from erstwhile Bengal. During the colonial rule, there were different laws for the administration of the hill areas of erstwhile Assam as well as the formerly princely states of Manipur and Tripura respectively. The Bengal Eastern Frontier Regulation, 1873 was enforced in the then Kamrup, Darrang, Nowgong, Sibsagar, Lakhimpur (Garo Hills), Khasi and Jaintia Hills, Naga Hills and Cachar to prohibit "all [citizens of India or any class of such citizens] or any persons residing in or passing through such districts from going beyond such line without a pass under the hand and seal of the Chief Executive Officer of such district or of such other officer as he may authorise to grant such pass; and the [state government] may, from time to time, cancel or vary such prohibition" (The Bengal Eastern Frontier Regulation, 1873, August 27, 1873). Today the regulation is locally known as the Inner Line Permit and is still effective in Arunachal Pradesh, Mizoram, Nagaland (apart from Dimapur) to restrict the entry of residents of other states of the country in those areas. There has been a renewed demand for the introduction of Inner Line Permit by several civil society social organisations in several states of the region as witnessed in Meghalaya and Manipur in recent times.

The region has a long history of difficult inter- and intra-regional connectivity. The larger population reside in the rural areas which are based on the agrarian economy. Agriculture is, therefore, the main source of their employment and livelihood. The food grains production is not sufficient to meet the consumption demand and hence is imported from outside. In fact, agriculture is heavily reliant upon seasonal rainfall. Furthermore, there is a negligible level of industrial and manufacturing activities. The growth in the tertiary sector is primarily due to the expansion of public administration with the state governments being the main employers. However, in the rapidly growing states of Punjab, Karnataka,

Kerala, Maharashtra or Tamil Nadu, there has been a relative decline in the agricultural sector against the services and manufacturing sectors.

The region has favourable human development indicators such as comparatively high literacy and low infant mortality. Despite these favourable development indicators, the region has not been able to build on these strengths and capture the potential. The standard of living of people lags behind the rest of the country. Also, the divergence in per capita income between the national average and the region shows a steady increase over the years. As a result, the region's population have been increasingly excluded from India's economic growth.

Additionally, several states have been affected by the insurgency movements and ethnic movements leading to extensive violence, along with population displacement and insecurity. The conflict impacts the direct and indirect costs which in turn affect livelihoods. Further, there are gaps in higher education, technical and vocational training in most states of the region, forcing many students to go to other parts of the country.

On the other hand, the economic liberalisation in the country and the consequent information technology development in prosperous parts of the country have created new jobs across sectors. As a result, a large number of people from across the country have migrated for employment to Bengaluru, Chennai, Delhi, Hyderabad, Pune and other cities. The lure of better job opportunities has attracted youth to such prosperous cities. In addition to this, there is the pull factor of a better environment for educational opportunities, with manifold choices for educational endeavours. In short, the main push factors that compelled youth out of the region have been the limited educational and job opportunities and the propensity of violent conflicts in the region, while the main pull factors are the availability of better educational and job opportunities in prosperous cities. Majority of them have migrated in search of better employment prospects and educational facilities.

Identity and Agency

In recent years, identity studies have emerged as a popular discipline. The factors that have contributed to its impressive growth over time coincide with the changing nature and structure of societies. Globalisation and neo-liberalism have paved the way for its advancement. Identity, a term which has been limited in its definition and closeted in its approach, has found a new meaning in the globalised world. The question of identity with the spectrum of 'Self' has extended itself into new domains of ideas. The term identity no longer finds its semblance and associations with culture, race and its artefacts alone. But, today, identity has concretised itself into varied representations, namely in the field of ethnicity, sexuality, sub-nationalities and gender.

It has been asserted that an individual has access to multiple identities and the cogency of each identity follows a hierarchal control system (Burke and Stets, 2009; 134). The bearing of each identity depends on the meaning it produces. In short, identity provides agency to an individual be it political, social or otherwise. This can be best exemplified in relation to the colonial exercise of imposing the culture, religion and language of the imperial powers over the colonised communities. This conversion can be best described as 'alchemic absorption' (Anderson, 2006; 15). The publication of Macaulay's Minutes (1835) in India or the heightened activities of Ku Klux Klan after the Civil War in America interestingly shared the same ideology of the 'white supremacy'. It enabled the white colonisers to perpetuate and justify their colonising mission under the premise of their 'superior culture'. The dialectic of cultural hegemony, despite geographical gaps, followed the same module in both nineteenth-century America and colonised India. Thereby, the idea of 'Self' in opposition to the 'Other' was regulated and introduced. In the context of Northeast India, the onset of Vaishnavism in seventeenth-century Manipur or the introduction of Christianity in Nagaland and Meghalaya had a resultant change in the lifestyle and cultural practices of the people. This raises the question of religious identity and highlights how nationalism and religion are deeply interconnected.

The concept of shared cultural and racial identity in the context of Northeast India has inherently shaped the politics of the region. The territorial identity of the region has largely been dictated by several tropes such as that of ethnicity, indigeneity and tribal identity. On the basis of such tropes, the de-territoralisation and re-terrtioralisation of the erstwhile demarcated colonised spaces have been classified. The reclaiming of cultural and religious history can be witnessed through the self-determination movements sweeping the region post-Independence of India. The linguistic and ethnic identity of the people has had a remarkable resurgence and revitalisation process over the recent years. The close ties between identity and politics in the region and the resultant consequences on the nation-building process is an important phenomenon that merits serious academic engagement.

The Book

The twelve essays in the book add valuable insights into different facets of colonial to post-colonial migration and the subsequent development of identity politics in Northeast India. The opening essay by M. Amarjeet Singh argues that India has to choose between taking firm action against illegal migration and strengthening bilateral relations with Bangladesh. It is most likely that the national policies shall prevail over local demands. But, the issue of illegal migration including the ongoing exercise to update on the National Register of Citizens has already caused a lot of confusion. Indeed, there is an absolute lack of clarity. The essay by Mrinal and Arobindo historically locate the nature of migration during the erstwhile kingdom of Tripura. They also discuss the several push-pull factors which have significantly influenced illegal Bangladeshi migration into Tripura. Focusing on Meghalaya, Anamika Deb Roy explores how the dominant ethnic group, especially those who derive their legitimacy and agency from the rubric of indigeneity and have over the years went on to vociferously exhibit their voice of difference towards whom they perceive as the 'others', 'outsider' or 'settler'. In her paper, Dolly Limbu examines the contours of Nepali identity in Manipur. The dearth of academic work on the community posits a serious impediment in understanding the community which has largely been excluded from the regional political discourses.

Rita Chakma maintains that the contemporary cross-border activity in the socio-religious arena, barring political and economic exchanges, cannot be termed as something new or alien developments. Rita traces the transformative streams in socio-religious life of the Chakmas, especially in the light of migration and cross-border development in recent decades.

Sneha Mishra, on the other hand, examines the causes behind the informal labour migration from Bihar to Assam and Sikkim. The paper further tries to understand the economic and social conditions that motivate their choice between Assam and Sikkim. Owing to factors such as geographical isolation, underdevelopment, economic backwardness and law and order problem, K.N. Tennyson in his paper, rightly observes that the northeastern region remains one of the most unexplored regions in the country. Huidrom Renuka's paper on out-migration from northeastern states looks at the emerging factors which influence young people to migrate. She also attempts to study the conditions of youth negotiating with insecurities, and disappointment, while living in Delhi. Sangeeta Angom and Stelin Singh explore the challenges of education in the

Northeast and projected education as a detrimental factor in ushering India's engagement with Southeast Asian countries. Ningthoujam Rameshchandra interestingly argues that Manipur has recently witnessed a heavy influx of immigrants. As a result, it has become an issue in space, settlement and resource distribution. It has largely invited the interest of civil society groups demanding appropriate policies in order to monitor the unregulated influx of immigrants. The paper by Immanuel Varte discusses migration in Jiribam district of Manipur. The paper talks about the strategic location of the said district as the strategic entry point of not only essential goods and services but also has attracted the in-flow of migrants. In the last essay, Dhiren Sadokpam argues that both the opponents and supporters of the Inner Line Permit system seem to have fallen trap to a self-imposed restriction and the overarching legal framework. Along the way, the finer details of separating the legal component from the political core have been blurred, rendering the current dispensation virtually helpless.

References

Anderson, Benedict. 2006. *Imagined Communities: Reflections on the Origin and Spread of Nationalism*, (Third Edition). New York: Verso Publications.

Berne Initiative. 2004. *Managing International Migration through International Cooperation: The International Agenda for Migration Management*. Berne: Berne Initiative.

Bohning, W.R. 1974. 'Immigration Policies of Western European Countries', *International Migration Review*, 8(2), 155-163.

Brennan, E.M. 1984. 'Irregular Migration: Policy Responses in Africa and Asia', *International Migration Review*, 18(3), 409-425.

Burke, Peter J. and Jan E. Stets. 2009. *Identity Theory*. New York: Oxford University Press.

Deshingkar, Priya and Grimm, Sven. 2004. *Voluntary Internal Migration: An Update*. London: Overseas Development Institute.

Douglas T. Gurak and Fe Caces. 2010. 'Migration networks and the shaping of migration systems', in Steven Vertovec, *Migration: Critical concepts in the social sciences*, Vol. 1. London and New York: Routledge.

Duvell, Franck. 2005. 'Irregular Migration: A Global Historical and Economic Perspective', in *Illegal Immigration in Europe: Beyond Control*, (ed.) Franck Duvell. Houndmills: Palgrave/MacMillan, 14-39.

Duvell, Franck. 2010. 'Irregular migration: a global, historical and economic perspective', in Steven Vertovec, (ed.), *Migration*, Volume 2. New York: Routledge, 289-310.

Government of Delhi. 2015. *Economic Survey of Delhi 2014-2015*. Delhi: Planning Department.

Hirst, Paul; Thomson, Grahame, and Bromley, Simon. 2009. *Globalization in Question* (Third Edition). Cambridge: Polity Press.

International Organisation for Migration. 2013. *World Migration Report 2013*. Geneva: International Organisation for Migration.

International Organization for Migration. 2009. *World Migration 2008: Managing Labour Mobility in the Evolving Global Economy*. Geneva: International Organization for Migration.

International Organization for Migration. 2015. *World Migration Report 2015: Migrants and Cities*: New Partnerships to Manage Mobility. Geneva: International Organization for Migration.

Lopreato, Joseph and Lawrence E. Hazelrigg. 2015. *Class, Conflict and Mobility: Theories and Studies of Class Structure* (Indian Reprint). Jaipur: Rawat Publications.

Massey D.S., *et al.* 1997. 'Theories of International Migration: A Review and Appraisal', *Population and Development Review* 19, 431-466.

Ministry of Development of North Eastern Region and North Eastern Council. 2008. *North Eastern Region Vision 2020*. Agartala.

Ministry of Health and Family Welfare, Government of India. 2009. *Health and Living Conditions in Eight Indian Cities, National Family Health Survey (NFHS-3) India 2005-06*. Mumbai: International Institute for Population Sciences.

Morris, Lydia. 1997. 'Globalization, Migration and the Nation-State: The Path to a Post-National Europe?' *The British Journal of Sociology*, 48(2), 192-209.

Portes, A. and Böröcz, J. 1989. 'Contemporary Immigration: Theoretical Perspectives on Its Determinants and Modes of Incorporation', *International Migration Review*, 23(3), 606-630.

Portes, A. 1978. 'Introduction: Toward a Structural Analysis of Illegal (Undocumented) Immigration', *International Migration Review*, 12(4), 469-484.

Rao, MSA. 1986. 'Some Aspects of Sociology of Migration in India', in MSA Rao, *Studies in Migration*. New Delhi: Manohar.

Sonia McKay, Eugenia Markova and Anna Paraskevopoulou. (2011). *Undocumented Workers' Transitions: Legal Status, Migration, and Work in Europe*. New York: Routledge.

Vertovec, Steven. 2010. *Migration: Critical concepts in the social sciences*, Vol. 1. London and New York: Routledge.

Vertovec, Steven. 2010. *Transnationalism*. London and New York: Routledge.

United Nations Development Programme. 2009. *Human Development Report 2009: Overcoming barriers: Human mobility and development*. New York: United Nations Development Programme.

Wood, William B. 1994. 'Forced Migration: Local Conflicts and International Dilemmas', *Annals of the Association of American Geographers* 84(4), 607-634.

1

Question of Citizenship

Difficulties and Hopes

M. Amarjeet Singh

The indigenous people of Northeast India have expressed serious concern about the adverse impact of illegal immigration from Bangladesh. However, India has to choose between taking firm action against illegal immigrants and that of promoting bilateral ties with Bangladesh. It is most likely that the national policies will ultimately prevail over local concerns. But, the issue of illegal migration including the ongoing exercise to update on the National Register of Citizens has already caused a lot of hope and confusion. Indeed, it is not clear how the exercise will serve its objectives. Their hopes were short-lived when the central government introduced the Citizenship (Amendment) Bill, 2016. The need of the hour is balancing the local concerns with that of the national policies. Migration is in itself a good thing – as long as the cultural identity of the indigenous people is not endangered.

Many countries follow different policies towards migration in which they adopt preferential treatment towards some migrant groups in contrast to others. Several sending countries discourage the migration of their high-skilled citizens into other countries but encourage unskilled ones to do so. Likewise, several receiving countries have adopted merit-based and need-based immigration. Despite such restrictions, many people continue to migrate voluntarily from one country to another through unauthorised means, including entering illegally or overstaying their visas/other travel documents (*see* Carretero, 2008, 1). Thus, many countries are simultaneously the source and recipient of illegal immigrants. In reality, illegal migration seems to have become an integral part of global migration (*see* Duvell, 2005, 16) as it happens in India, the United States and European countries.

The rapid social transformation took place in Assam along with the advent and consolidation of British rule in the nineteenth century as tea plantation, coal mining and oil exploration began. Rail lines were also constructed. Additionally, in order to serve their economic and geo-political interests, the administrative boundaries were redrawn several times. Assam was administratively attached to Bengal Presidency for about half a century, during 1826-1873. In 1874, Assam became a separate province along with Cachar, Sylhet and Goalpara districts of Bengal. Administrative boundaries were redrawn again in 1905 in which eastern parts of Bengal and Assam became East Bengal and Assam (with Dhaka as the capital), and Bengal, respectively. However, it was dissolved in 1911. Thus, Assam became a preferred destination for migration resulting in the increase in the numerical strength of the immigrants. The immigrants comprised both job-seeking and the land-seeking farm settlers (Nag, 2018, 88).

Being the earliest recipient of western education and their long association with colonial administrators, the people of Bengal occupied a crucial role in the administration of Assam. This naturally facilitated in popularising and consolidating the use of Bengali language in the spheres of administration and school education. Ultimately, Bengali became the language of Courts of Justices and of the government schools during 1837-1874 (*see* Report of the Administration of Bengal, 1871-72, Part I). It was a controversial step for overruling the wishes of the indigenous inhabitants of Assam. These were done in 'the interest of tea plantation and trade' (Nag, 2018, 87). Assamese was recognised as the language of courts and schools in 1874 by retaining Bengali script.

The Partition of India into India and Pakistan was a painful exercise which affected the lives of millions of people, as Muslims in India fled towards Pakistan and Hindus in Pakistan fled towards India. Subsequently, the language became a powerful tool for political mobilisation in the newly independent India which led to the creation of linguistic states such as Andhra (later Andhra Pradesh) (*see* Singh and Pani, 2012). In a similar manner, a movement for recognition of Assamese language as the official language started in Assam which ultimately led to the passing of the Assam Official Language Act, 1960, in which Assamese became 'the language to be used for official purposes' of the state. The Act was opposed by different communities (*see* Grover, 1997, 200). Furthermore, the Gauhati University (one of the oldest universities in the country) resolved in 1972 to introduce Assamese as the language of undergraduate education in colleges under its jurisdiction. The resolution was also opposed by several communities in which the Barak valley even demanded a union territory to be carved out of Assam.

During the liberation struggle of Bangladesh in 1971 (it resulted in the breakup of Pakistan as East Pakistan turned into Bangladesh), more than 10 million refugees fled to India (UNHCR, 2000, 61). A large number of them reportedly did not return to their new country. In addition, many more poor people have migrated from different parts of Bangladesh to different parts of India. Now seasonal and circular migration is taking place in which the preferred destinations are Barak valley of Assam and West Bengal. What is pertinent to know is why it is a one-way migration towards India?

Bangladesh is one of the most densely populated countries in the world with the land-man ratio of 0.6 hectares in 2010. The country is regularly affected by natural disasters including floods, droughts and cyclones. India which is several times bigger surrounded Bangladesh by about 4096.7 km long land border. India has a comparatively lower population density which is further lower in the northeastern region. Experts have predicted the rise of sea level by nearly eight feet by 2100 and about 50 feet by 2300 if greenhouse gas emissions remain high (*Hindustan Times*, October 9, 2018, 1). If this actually happens more people are expected to come to India.

Table 1.1: Population density of Bangladesh, India and Northeast India

Country/Region	*Population density*	
	1961	2017
Bangladesh	381	1,265
India	154	450
Northeast India	102*	159**

Source: World Bank, (2018).

* Population density of undivided Assam (1961 Census)

** Calculated from 2011 Census of India.

As the language crisis receded, migration again attracted public attention in Assam which finally led to a popular people's movement known as the Assam movement which began in the late-1970s. It was followed by the signing of an agreement, popularly known as the Assam Accord, in 1985 in which the central government promised to fulfil the main demands of the movement including taking steps for identification and deportation of the 'non-citizens', officially known as the 'foreigners' from Assam. It recognised March 24, 1971, as the cutoff date for the identification of foreigners. The agreement also promised to take the necessary measures to protect the linguistic and cultural identity of the 'Assamese people'.

Who knows the number?

No one knows how many people had actually come to India in general and Assam in particular at different times, perhaps between 1947 and 1971. There is no way of knowing it also except for official and unofficial estimates which are merely guesswork. These estimates are confusing and their reliability is doubtful. According to several academic and activist literature, unabated migration from Bangladesh is one of the main causes of higher population growth in Assam during the major part of the 20th century. Large-scale immigration from Bangladesh is also been considered as the 'silent demographic invasion', 'conspiracy', 'main problem', 'cultural threat' and 'security threat' (*see* Ministry of Home Affairs, 2013; Kumar, 2006; Government of India, 2001). They also referred to the higher growth of the Muslim population than the average population growth. This has been extensively debated for a long time without coming to any decisive conclusion. However, former Assam Chief Minister Tarun Gogoi considered illiteracy, not illegal migration, as the main reason for the growth of Muslim population in the state. Muslims have reportedly become the majority in several districts of Assam (*see* Rajkhowa, 2013).

We have also heard about the fraudulently enrolling of suspected illegal immigrants during the preparation of electoral rolls in Assam. For example, during the revision of the electoral rolls of Mangaldoi Lok Sabha constituency in 1979, about 70,000 complaints were registered within a short period. The Election Commission of India upheld about 64.28 per cent of the complaints of unlawful inclusion in the electoral rolls (*see* Mohanty, 2008, 43). This arguably became the trigger for the Assam movement.

The Assam movement brought forth new problems as several ethnic groups started reasserting their distinctness from the larger (Assamese) ethnic group. Notable among them is the Bodos who do not want to be identified with the 'Assamese people' as stated in the Assam accord. The Bodos were initially mobilised in their demand for the recognition of their language as the medium of instruction, and subsequently followed by the demand for their own script. Once their language became an associate official language, the movement for a separate state started (Singh, 2004).

Leaders of the movement also launched the political party Asom Gana Parishad (AGP) while their opponents launched the United Minorities Front (UMF). The former won the state legislative elections held in 1985 and 1996, respectively while the latter failed to make any significant impact politically.[1]

How immigration is problematic in Northeast India?

The immigrants are engaged in a variety of works which the indigenous inhabitants regarded as not lucrative and hence not interested. They provide cheap labour and loyal workforce. When a significant number of immigrants have started doing certain occupations, those occupations became 'immigrant jobs' which are socially undesirable for native workers. The native workers would like to do 'native jobs' and are less inclined towards 'immigrant jobs'. The distinction between immigrant and native jobs came from the presence of immigrants, not from the characteristics of occupations (Bohning, 1974, 155-163).

The indigenous inhabitants of the region are not against immigration. However, they are worried about large-scale immigration because of the fear of being outnumbered by the immigrants and their descendants. This is a legitimate concern since most of the indigenous communities are numerically small and are confined to specific territory. In addition, their insecurity has been further reinforced by the fact that the immigrant communities control wholesale and retail trade in almost all the towns and cities of the region such as Guwahati, Imphal and Shillong.

A study conducted in Nagaland found that two-thirds of respondents considered the availability of jobs and aversion to manual labour by the indigenous inhabitants responsible for immigration into Nagaland. Several respondents alleged that the traditional institution of Chiefship patronised immigration since the village Chiefs needed immigrants in order to perform agricultural works in the newly established villages (Singh, 2009).[2] But, the presence of a large number of immigrants in different places is perceived as a social threat by the indigenous inhabitants. Immigration is thought to have contributed to rapid population growth especially in areas bordering Assam. The law-enforcement agencies were helpless in dealing with the situation because most immigrants have already registered as voters and other beneficiaries of public services.[3] The study (Singh, 2009) also confirmed reports of the prevalence of intermarriage between immigrants and indigenous inhabitants. A local student group Naga Students'

Federation had tried to restrict such intermarriage without much success. Now, a little-known Sumia community has reportedly emerged. It is a sensitive and emotional issue because a section of the indigenous inhabitants refused to acknowledge it. During my fieldwork in Dimapur, most people refused to discuss it. My well-wishers advised me not to talk about it. Even the local leaders were hesitant to talk and mention about Sumias. In 2002, the then Chief Minister S.C. Jamir had denied newspaper reports that he had ever talked about the said community. He had clarified, "I said illegal immigrants are mostly found in Dimapur and Niuland. Some Bangladeshis had married Naga women and vice-versa, thereby making the whole matter more complicated. The assumption that I am insulting a certain tribe is unfortunate and uncalled for" (*Sentinel*, Guwahati, April 19, 2002).

Table 1.2: Language and mother tongues with speakers' strength, 2011

Major		*Small*	
Name of language	*Speakers' strength*	*Name of language*	*Speakers' strength*
Telugu	8,09,12,459	Manipuri	17,60,913
Tamil	6,88,88,839	Kokbarak	9,17,900
Odia	3,40,59,266	Adi	1,10,307
Marathi	8,28,01,140	Ao	1,19,549
Bhojpuri	5,05,79,447	Dimasa	1,37,187
Bengali	9,61,77,835	Khasi	10,37,964
Assamese	1,48,16,414	Bodo	14,54,547

Source: Census of India 2011, LANGUAGE, New Delhi: Office of the Registrar General, India, 2011

Let us briefly discuss the situation of Tripura. Like in Assam, a large number of East Bengal refugees fled to Tripura at the time of the Partition. They were compelled to come to Tripura. About 6.09 lakh refugees were reportedly rehabilitated during 1947-1971. This excluded another 1.8 lakh 'unofficial' refugees of the period 1951-1961 (Debbarma, 2006: 406). The refugees were initially accommodated at different transit camps and later allotted land and financial assistance to settle permanently (Debbarma, 1996: 19). In due course of time, the refugees also set up cooperative societies to purchase more land for settlement (Bhaumik and Bhattacharya, 2005: 225). As a consequence, Tripura's population grew at a faster rate of about 76.86 per cent during 1951-1961. Again, a large number of refugees also came during the liberation movement of Bangladesh. The population growth was higher than any other part of the country during 1961-1991. As a result, the Bengali-speaking population had outnumbered the indigenous inhabitants and hence became the politically dominant community in Tripura. As a result, Bengali and English became the official languages in 1964, while Kokborok, the language of the Boroks, became an additional official language in 1979 (currently, Bengali and Kokborok are the official languages). The indigenous communities blamed the successive state governments for ignoring their language as well as imposing the learning of Bengali upon them. They were gradually alienated from their ancestral land starting with 300 sq miles of the 1950 sq miles of reserved land which was taken over for the settlement of the refugees and moreover they could not match with the newcomers in shrewdness. This became the main driver of insurgency including a bloody riot in 1983 (Government of Tripura, 2007: 106). Numerically smaller communities of Tripura and Assam have suffered immensely after the partition of the erstwhile Bengal.

With the aim of controlling and identifying illegal immigrants from Assam, several measures have already been adopted by the Indian state. Surprisingly such policies were not meant for Tripura. In 1950, the central government enacted The Immigrants (Expulsion from Assam) Act, 1950 "for the expulsion of certain immigrants from Assam." The statement of objects and reasons of the said Act says,

> During the last few months a serious situation had arisen from the immigration of a very large number of East Bengal residents into Assam. Such large migration is disturbing the economy of the province, besides giving rise to a serious law and order problem. The Bill seeks to confer necessary powers on the central government to deal with the situation (*see* 'Memoruam to the Prime Minister of India', February 2, 1980 by Prafulla Mahanta, President of AASU, and Brigu Kr. Phukan, Secretary of AASU)

Based on the Census report of 1951, the National Register of Citizens was prepared in 1951 containing information on relevant particulars of each and every person enumerated. The Register contains about 80 lakh Indians living in Assam. The central government issued a statutory order known as the Foreigners (Tribunal) Order in 1964 in order to constitute Foreigners' Tribunals.[4] In 1983, the Parliament passed the Illegal Migrants (Determination by Tribunals) Act, applicable to Assam only, to identify and deport the non-citizens while the Foreigner Act, 1946 was in force in other parts of the country. Under the said Act, a foreigner is defined as those who illegally settled down in Assam on and after March 25, 1971, and the onus of proof lies with the complainant. On the other hand, the Foreigners Act puts the onus on the accused to prove his/her Indian nationality. In 1983, IMDTs were set up. While IMDTs looked into cases of suspected foreigners of the post-March 25, 1971 stream, the Foreigners' Tribunals were entrusted with the responsibility of disposing of cases pertaining to pre-March 25, 1971 stream of suspected foreigners. But, according to one Assam minister, only 219 foreigners were deported from the state between 2001 to November 2010, while over Rs. 33 crores were spent on the Foreigners' Tribunals.[5]

When the Supreme Court declared the Illegal Migrants (Determination by Tribunals) Act as *ultra vires* in 2005 for inability to identify and deport foreigners, the 21 IMDTs were replaced by 21 Foreigners' Tribunals. However, most of the 'detected foreigners' were untraceable. Detention centres have also been set up in order to restrict their movement.[6] Further, the construction of fencing, roads and floodlighting along the India-Bangladesh border has been undertaken.[7] But the border remains highly porous as there are forests, lowlands, rivers and human settlements.

However, these measures have not been very effective. Moreover, the distinction between Bangladeshis and Indians is not easily distinguishable. Thus, the indigenous inhabitants of the region wanted other measures to protect their cultural and political interests including preferential policies in education and employment. One of the most common demands is the implementation of the inner line permit (or similar measure) in order to restrict the entry of the residents from other states of the country. Such a mechanism is currently being enforced in the state of Arunachal Pradesh, Nagaland and Mizoram.[8] Recently I have had an opportunity to moderate a panel discussion on inner line permit in Delhi, and during the discussion, I was convinced that the purpose of inner line permit during the colonial times was different from what it is being projected today. In the past, the prime motive was to safeguard the tea plantation in the plain and cornered the hill people into enclaves and restricted trade and communication with other communities along the foothills. However, it was portrayed as a mechanism to safeguard the customs and livelihoods of the hill people. Today it is merely a travel permit as it is in Nagaland, Arunachal Pradesh and Mizoram. Several civil society groups including the All Assam Students' Union wanted a special law whereby 'outsiders' cannot become owners of land in the region. In 2018, the Manipur legislative assembly has passed the Manipur People's Bill 2018 and is awaiting the approval of the central government.

National Register of Citizens

The National Register of Citizens is a register prepared way back in 1951 which contains names of Indian citizens based on the particulars of all the persons enumerated during the 1951 Census. The register is being presently updated to include those persons (or the descendants of those persons) whose names appear in the original register or electoral rolls up to the midnight of March 24, 1971, or any other related documents. A person can seek inclusion in the register if there is the existence of his or her name in the pre-1971 period and proving linkage with those persons who appeared in the original register (*see* Government of Assam, 2018).

The process of updating the register has been delayed for over thirty years due to the lack of political will (Barooah, 2012). Finally, the Supreme Court of India in 2014 directed the authorities to take note of the progress of the implementation and to conform to a time schedule.[9] Assam is the only state in India where the registrar is being updated, with March 24, 1971, as the cut-off date, to include names of genuine citizens. Four categories of people: (a) D-voters, (b) their descendants, (c) people whose cases were pending at different Foreigners Tribunals, and (d) their offspring were not included in the list. The exercise is based on the Assam Accord and hence those who had entered Assam after March 24, 1971, will be considered as an illegal immigrant.

The exercise generates endless excitements, hopes and apprehensions. Some people are optimistic, some are pessimistic. The first draft which was made public in December 2017 confirmed the citizenship of 1.90 crore people.[10] The draft register was finally published on July 30, 2018, with 2.9 crore people leaving out 40.07 lakh people who could not produce valid documents. The exercise has underscored the importance of better documentation to establish an individual's Indian nationality. When the draft register was published, the media and civil society based primarily outside Assam have generated a lot of speculations as suggested by the newspaper headlines which I have randomly selected at the time of the publication. The exercise had been wrongly projected as a ploy to divide the people along religious lines. Despite the negative publicity, the exercise has been smooth. Misleading narratives were produced by civil society and media outside Assam.

For instance, the BBC (July 30, 2018) carried an article entitled 'Assam register: Four million risk losing India citizenship' in which it says that "Many Bengalis — a linguistic minority in Assam — are worried they will be deported en masse." The paper also says that the exercise is being "used as a pretext for a two-pronged attack — by Hindu nationalists and Assamese hardliners — on the state's Bengali community, a large portion of whom are Muslims."[11] This is a misleading report. There were similar reports: 'India Assam: Will four million people really be deported?' (BBC, August 9, 2018), 'What happens to India's four million 'stateless' people?' (BBC, July 30, 2018), 'Indian officials say Assam register does not target Muslims' (BBC, August 3, 2018), 'India strips four million people of citizenship in Assam as Modi's BJP 'targets' Muslim minority' (*The Telegraph*, UK, July 30, 2018), 'On fire, a melting pot' (*The Telegraph*, Kolkata, July 29, 2018), and 'The 4007707 human question' (*The Telegraph*, Kolkata, July 31, 2018).

The ruling Bharatiya Janata Party (BJP) used the occasion to attack opposition parties to take a clear stand on the issue and not indulge in vote bank politics. West Bengal Chief Minister Mamta Banerjee accused the BJP of resorting to 'divide and rule' politics.[12] She even accused the BJP-led central government of hatching a conspiracy to drive out Bengalis from Assam by excluding their names from the National Register of Citizens.[13] However, there were balanced reporting on the matter such as 'For four million, another chance to make it to National Register of Citizens' (*The Hindu*, August 11, 2018), 'Not just Muslims, even Hindu Bengalis left out of Assam's citizen list', (*Hindustan Times*, August 1, 2018), and 'Fear and hope on Day One as those out of NRC begin to file their claims', (*Indian Express*, August 11, 2018).

When the draft register was released, the neighbouring states of Assam reportedly took extra security measures fearing the influx of immigrants who do not find their names in the register. Several civil society groups of the region had even demanded a similar exercise to be conducted in other states of the region. On a lighter note, several politicians called for a similar exercise in other parts of the country without ascertaining the importance of the current exercise. However, several northeastern states wanted a similar exercise to be conducted in their states.

Identification and no question of deportation: The draft register is not meant to deport any person from Assam because those unable to enlist their names in the register can make claims and objections. After completion of the disposal of claims and objections, the final registers shall be published. So we have to wait and watch rather than jump into a premature conclusion. However, for an ordinary person, the issue of citizenship is not only troublesome but may also be expensive affair as the entire process involves seeking legal assistance.[14] For example, D-voter is a category of citizenship in which 'D' stands for 'doubtful'. For a D-voter getting clearance for the removal of his/her name from the electoral roll and get inclusion in the register will be an arduous task. Thus, the exercise will add to the suffering of many people especially belonging to poor and marginal groups. If they fail to get their names enlisted in the register they would suffer harassment and discrimination. They will be deprived of basic services. It has been recognised that good governance is essential for sustainable development, both economic and social. Any meaningful discussion on good governance is likely to focus on how to bridge the gap between the government and the citizens. Most people depend on the government for different types of essential services in their day-to-day lives. If the public services are delivered on time it enhances the people's perceptions towards their governments. However, those people would be deprived of these services, at least temporarily.

The exercise may be possible to identify illegal immigrants in Assam but won't be possible to deport them back to Bangladesh. The two countries do not have any agreement to deport illegal immigrants from each other's side. Furthermore, Bangladesh won't accept them. It is not easy going because Bangladesh never acknowledges the presence of its citizens in India. It had even accused India of evicting Bengali-speaking Muslims by branding them as Bangladeshis. Bangladesh is least concerned about the illegal migration from its soil into India.[15]

On its part, India won't be able to take firm action against illegal immigrants. First of all, there are close historical and cultural links between India and Bangladesh. For India, maintaining cordial relations with Bangladesh ought to be more important than forcibly deporting illegal immigrants. In this context, Assam Chief Minister Sarbananda Sonowal had reportedly stated after the publication of the first draft of the register: "The issue of deportation will come later. First, our target is to segregate the foreigners. What steps we will take against them will come next.... For almost 40 years, our people have been living in a state of confusion and uncertainty. The NRC will end this. It is a win-win situation for everybody. Nobody will question anybody's citizenships" (Kalita, 2018). In fact, this is easier to say than to do.

Until the final draft was published, an individual can enrol in the register to prove his/her Indian citizenship by providing one of the 15 identified documents. But, the agency undertaking the exercise proposed to drop five documents (such as NRC 1951, voters' lists, refugee registration certificate, citizenship certificate, and ration card — all issued before March 24, 1971) for filing claims and objections by those whose names have left out. The officials apprehended attempt to enrol illegal immigrants in the register 'through forgery' belonging to the five documents, and in the process, the five documents could be misused. They even alleged that some pro-immigrant groups who objected to the exclusion of the five documents were trying to bring illegal immigrants into Assam. However, those objecting to the dropping of the five documents claimed that many people would face extreme difficulties in the process of filing claims.[16] However, the Supreme Court on November 1, 2018, lifted the stay on use of five documents. The court asked the authorities for an additional layer of scrutiny in the use of five documents.[17] The court also extended the deadline for filing of claims and objections and the digitisation of the relevant documents.

The official associated with the exercise rightly pointed out that such a massive exercise cannot be error-free. They also admitted that the possibility of inclusion of foreign nationals in the register cannot be ruled out. The authorities would have a tough time in the identification of the ineligible names. For instance, the names of those who were declared as foreigners by the Foreigners' Tribunals have to be deleted from the register. Some people did not apply for inclusion of their names.[18] Certain doubtful cases have been included, while others have been excluded. Thus, the officials have suggested re-verification in certain cases and places.

Political parties in Assam are divided over the issue of illegal migration and accused of indulging in the politics of minority/majority appeasement for vote-bank. We have come across several media reports in which the BJP and AGP accused Congress party of indulging in minority appeasement. On the other hand, the Congress party has always accused the BJP of practising communal politics. Congress leader Tarun Gogoi had alleged that the purpose of NRC update has failed because of 'improper implementation' and 'politicisation'. According to him, the NRC and the Citizenship (Amendment) Bill is a contradiction.[19] Similarly, public opinion is also divided. When the Illegal Migrants (Determination by Tribunals) Act was overruled by the Supreme Court, several Muslim groups expressed fear that it would lead to harassment of the members of the community on the pretext of the identification of the foreigners. On the other hand, organisations like All Assam Students' Union welcomed the verdict. When the first draft of the National Register of Citizens was published, the BJP had asked the opposition parties to take a clear stand on the issue and not indulge in vote bank politics.

As there are different stakeholders on the issue of illegal migration into the country and hence each of them looks at the National Register of Citizenship differently. Some stakeholders are worried that the exercise is unlikely to identify illegal immigrants and hence could not fulfil the purpose of the Assam Accord. In fact, the exercise seems to have unsettled political parties. Some stakeholders wanted to manipulate National Register of Citizens as it is not moving in the direction they had anticipated, but they are not able to do so.

Related to the issue of availing basic services is the prospect of corrupt practices. Already we are aware that corruption is another hindrance in the implementation of several measures because the aspiring migrants can easily fraudulently acquire identity documents such as ration cards, birth certificates, driving licenses and voters' identity cards. There is no guarantee that the National Register of Citizens is free from corrupt practices?

The National Register of Citizens should have been more effective if updated earlier. It is also not clear whether it would continue to be a valid identification paper for official purposes. If so, the agency overseeing the exercise shall be expected to remain as a permanent official agency because anyone having valid documents have to be enlisted in the register. Finally, in spite of many challenges, the National Register of Citizen will act as a deterrent for aspiring migrants from across the border through illegal means. Now, the names updated in the register will be required to cross-check with the electoral rolls. It is not clear to deal with illegal immigrants after the exercise.

Citizenship (Amendment) Bill, 2016

The main purpose of updating the National Register of Citizens has been contradicted by the Citizenship (Amendment) Bill 2016. During an election rally near Silchar in Assam in 2014, the BJP leader Narendra Modi, now the Prime Minister, promised to accommodate the Hindus from Bangladesh in India if BJP won the elections and gets into power. According to him, there are two types of Bangladeshi immigrants in Assam: (a) immigrants who are part of a 'political conspiracy' forming a crucial vote-bank, and (b) immigrants who are harassed in Bangladesh. Some people alleged that the party has been unfavourable towards the first category of immigrants but wanted to accommodate the latter category of immigrants.[20]

The Citizenship (Amendment) Bill, 2016, which was introduced in the Lok Sabha in 2016, seeks to amend the Citizenship Act, 1955 to change among others the definition of illegal migrants. The following provisions have been inserted in the proposed amendment:

> Provided that persons belonging to minority communities, namely, Hindus, Sikhs, Buddhists, Jains, Parsis and Christians from Afghanistan, Bangladesh and Pakistan, who have been exempted by the Central Government by or under clause (c) of sub-section (2) of section 3 of the Passport (Entry into India) Act, 1920 or from the application of the provisions of the Foreigners Act, 1946 or any order made thereunder, shall not be treated as illegal migrants for the purposes of this Act.
>
> Provided that for the persons belonging to minority communities, namely, Hindus, Sikhs, Buddhists, Jains, Parsis and Christians from Afghanistan, Bangladesh and Pakistan, the aggregate period of residence or service of a Government in India as required under this clause shall be read as "not less than six years" in place of "not less than eleven years".[21]

According to this Bill, the Hindus, Sikhs, Buddhists, Jains, Parsis and Christians from Afghanistan, Bangladesh and Pakistan shall not be treated as illegal immigrants in India. The Bill received a mixed response: some groups welcome the move and other groups oppose the move. But it was opposed in Assam and other Northeastern states by several political parties and civil society fearing that the region would become a 'dumping ground' for Hindus from Bangladesh. The indigenous inhabitants of the region are against it. Amidst this anxiety in the region, the Union Home Ministry has already empowered 16 collectors across seven states namely, Gujarat, Madhya Pradesh, Maharashtra, Chhattisgarh, Rajasthan, Uttar Pradesh and Delhi to register members of 'persecuted minorities' from Pakistan, Afghanistan and Bangladesh living in India without valid legal documents as Indian citizens under the Citizenship Act, 1955. The notification came at a time when the Citizenship (Amendment) Bill, 2016 has been strongly opposed in the Northeast. Many argued that the move will help illegal immigrants to enter Assam and other Northeast states from other parts of the country after getting Indian citizenship from other states.[22] The Bill was ultimately passed by the Lok Sabha but has not been tabled in the Rajya Sabha.

Conclusion

Although we should have the right to migrate freely but we cannot simply migrate freely anymore. As a result, we cannot simply migrate freely from one country to another. Northeast India is not against immigration but there is a genuine concern about the social impact of large scale immigration into the region. Migration is in itself a good thing – as long as the cultural identity of the indigenous people is not endangered. This is because the region is inhabited by a large number of numerically smaller groups. The task of updating the National Register of Citizens has been welcomed by the people of the region hoping that it will discourage unabated immigration. Their hopes were short-lived when the central government introduced the Citizenship (Amendment) Bill, 2016. The people of the region were united in their opposition to the Bill. If the Bill is passed and becomes a law, Hindu immigrants who are illegally staying in the country will cease to be illegal immigrants. This will have an adverse impact in the region in general and Assam in particular. The movement against illegal migration in Assam does not favour one group of immigrants against others on the basis of religion. The Bill distinguishes the immigrants on the basis of religion. The Bill has not been a concern in other parts of the country as it used to be in the Northeast. There is a clear manifestation of the conflict between local interests and larger national interest. This underscores how the state welcomes some while at the same time excludes some others. However, even if the Bill does not become a law, some groups are always preferred in the country.

Notes

1. Although the UMF had already become irrelevant, the All India Democratic United Front is said to be its reincarnation.
2. It was told during the author's fieldwork in Dimapur (Nagaland) on February 18, 2005.
3. Fieldwork by the author with policemen posted at Khatkhati on the Assam-Nagaland border of November 11, 2008.
4. The Foreigner Tribunals set up after 1964 became dysfunctional between December 1969 and March 1973 on the ground that 'most of the infiltrators had been deported'. Interestingly, the tribunals were reconstituted in 1979.
5. 'Rs 33 cr for deporting 219 foreigners', *Assam Tribune*, February 11, 2011.
6. Detention Centres were set up at Goalpara, Kokrajhar and Silchar.
7. The India-Bangladesh border touches Assam, West Bengal, Meghalaya, Tripura and Mizoram.

8. Any Indian nationals who wish to visit Arunachal Pradesh, Mizoram and Nagaland (except Dimapur town) require a permit known as inner-line permit issued by the competent state officials to enter those territories. Implemented under the East Bengal Frontier Regulation Act, 1873, during the days of the British, its intention is to prohibit any subject living outside the area from living or moving therein so as to keep the demographic profile of those territories intact.
9. *See* Judgment of December 17, 2014, In the Supreme Court of India, Civil Original Jurisdiction, Writ Petition (Civil) No. 562 of 2012, No. 274 of 2009 & No. 876 of 2014).
10. 'Final draft of Assam's citizens list leaves out 4m; govt says no genuine Indian should have any fear,' *The Telegraph*, July 30, 2018.
11. 'Assam register: Four million risk losing India citizenship', BBC, July 30, 2018, Available online https://www.bbc.com/news/world-asia-india-45002549 (accessed on October 14, 2018).
12. 'Mamata Banerjee, 'With NRC they're trying to divide people, there'll be bloodbath and civil war in country', *Indian Express*, July 31, 2018.
13. 'A ploy to drive out Bengalis: Mamata', *Times of India*, January 4, 2018, p. 11.
14. "Doubtful Voter are those persons who are identified during electoral roll revision as D Voters, cases of which are pending with the Foreigners Tribunals or as declared as foreigners by the Tribunal. D Voters can apply for inclusion of their names in the updated NRC. However, a D Voter's name will only be included in NRC after getting clearance from the Foreigners Tribunals and on removal of their names as D Voter from the electoral roll." *See* Government of Assam, (2018).
15. I have had the opportunity to meet several academicians and scholars from Bangladesh in Delhi.
16. R. Dutta Choudhury, (2018), 'Efforts on to include names of immigrants in NRC,' *Assam Tribune*, October 28.
17. Mahapatra, Dhananjay, (2018), "NRC: Use of 5 Documents allowed by SC," *Times of India*, November 2, p.14.
18. R. Dutta Choudhury, (2018), 'Attempts being made to discredit NRC: Hajela,' *The Assam Tribune*, August 5.
19. *See* 'Gogoi demands NRC for entire country,' *Assam Tribune*, August 27, 2018
20. 'Narendra Modi says Hindu migrants from Bangladesh must be accommodated,' *India Today*, February 25, 2014.
21. Lok Sabha, (2016), The Citizenship (Amendment) Bill, 2016 (Bill No. 172 of 2016).
22. *See* 'Centre to make Assam a dumping ground for Bangladeshis: All Assam Students' Union (AASU),' *The Sentinel*, October 29, 2018.

References

Bhaumik, Subir and J. Bhattacharya. 2005. 'Autonomy in Northeast: The Hills of Tripura and Mizoram,' in Ranabir Samaddar (ed.), *The Politics of Autonomy: the Indian Experiences*. New Delhi: Sage Publication, 216-241.

Bohning, W.R. 1974. 'Immigration Policies of Western European Countries,' *International Migration Review*, 8(2), 155-163.

Debbarma, Sukhendu. 2006. 'Peace Accords in Tripura: Background and Analysis,' in Prasenjit Biswas and C Joshua Thomas, (eds.), *Peace in North East India: Meaning, Metaphor and Method*. New Delhi: Regency Publication, 405-424.

Government of Assam. 2018. *In a Nutshell*. Guwahati: Office of the State Coordinator of National Registration (NRC), Assam.

Government of Assam. 2018. *D Voters*. Guwahati: Office of the State Coordinator of National Registration (NRC), Assam.

Government of Tripura. 2007. *Tripura Human Development Report 2007*. Agartala: Government of Tripura.

Grover, Verinder (ed.). 1997. *Pressure Groups and Politics of Influence*. New Delhi: Deep & Deep Publications.

Kalita, Prabin. 2018. 'Those not in NRC won't get constitutional rights: CM', *Times of India*, January 1, 2018.

Kalyan Barooah. 2012. 'Concern over influx from Bangladesh', *Assam Tribune*, November 9.

Nag, Sajal. 2018. 'Assamese nationality question', in Bhagat Oinam and Dhiren A, Sadokpam (eds.), *Northeast India: A Reader*. Oxon and New Delhi: Routledge.

Press Information Bureau. 2014. *Asylum to Foreigners fleeing Religious Persecution*, December 17. New Delhi: Government of India, Ministry of Home Affairs.

Rajkhowa, J.P. 2013. 'Some Disturbing Trends from 2011 Census Report,' *The Sentinel*, 5 January.

Singh, M, Amarjeet. 2009. *A Study on Illegal Immigration into North-East India: The Case of Nagaland*. New Delhi: Institute for Defence Studies and Analyses.

Singh, M. Amarjeet and Narendar Pani. 2012. 'Territories beyond geography: an alternative approach to the demands for new states in India,' *Commonwealth & Comparative Politics*, 50(1), 121-140

Talukdar, Sushanta. 2014. 'Only Centre can decide asylum issue: Assam,' *The Hindu*, August 7.

UNHCR. 2000. The State of the World's Refugees 2000: Fifty Years of Humanitarian Action. Oxford University Press.

World Bank. 2018. Population density (people per sq. km of land area). Washington: World Bank.

2

Understanding Push-Pull Factors of Migration from Bangladesh to Tripura

A Study on Sepahijala District

Mrinal Kanti Deb and *Arobindo Mahato*

There was a large-scale migration into Tripura even before joining the Union of India and the process is continuing. The study emphasised on push-pull factors of illegal Bangladeshi migration (after 25 March 25, 1971) into Tripura, and also found out the religious nexus within the push-pull factors.

Migration, as a global trend, will continue to do so in the near future. Migration involves the (more or less) permanent movement of people across symbolic or political and administrative boundaries into new areas (Gordon, 1998). Migration into Tripura is neither post-independent phenomenon nor during the Bangladesh freedom movement. The path for migration was set, by the erstwhile Maharaja of Tripura Ratna Manikya, in the thirteenth century by bringing educated Bengalis in order to assist the kingdom's administration (Bhaumik, 2012). Before the Independence, it was the economic reason which fuelled immigration of Bengali settlers into Tripura. However, after Independence, the political disturbance became the main reason for migration (Bhattacharyya, 1988). For instance, between the years 1939 to 1946 'several thousand' immigrants entered Tripura due to communal riots in Raipur, Dacca, Noakhali and Chandra (De, 2013). Similarly, during the Bangladesh liberation war, another phase of influx took place. However, according to the Indira-Mujib Treaty, those who had entered from East Pakistan (now Bangladesh) to India up to 24 March 1971, India took the responsibility of them. Hence, the influx from Bangladesh to Tripura after this cut-off date cannot be considered a refugee (Deb & Mahato, 2017). According to the agreement signed between the Government of Tripura and the All Tripura Tiger Force (ATTF), the former insurgent group, in 1993 promised to take action "in respect of sending back all Bangladesh foreign nationals who have come to Tripura after 25 March, 1971 and are not in possession of valid documents authorising their presence in Tripura" (*see* The Memorandum of Settlement between the Government of Tripura and the ATTF). The agreement is popularly known as the ATTF Accord. It included 16 promises to be fulfilled by the State Government (Mahato & Deb, 2017). The insurgent group, under the leadership of Ranjit Debbarma, gave up the path of armed struggle and violence and came to normal life. Therefore, in the case of Assam and Tripura the definition is clear: in spite of having all valid documents if any person has entered after 25 March 1971 will be treated as an illegal immigrant.

Tripura has the longest border share (856 km) with Bangladesh among the northeastern states. The state has a population of 3,671,032 with 14.75 per cent growth as compared to 2001 census (Census of India, 2011). Presently, Hindus constitute almost 83.4 per cent proportion followed by Muslims with almost 8.6 per cent proportion (*see* Table 2.1).

Table 2.1: Religious Composition of Tripura (in per cent)

Religion	*1991*	*2001*	*2011*
Hindu	86.4	85.62	83.40
Muslim	7.12	7.95	8.60
Christian	1.6	3.20	4.35
Sikh	–	0.04	0.03
Buddhist	4.6	3.09	3.41
Jain	-	0.01	0.02
Other religion	0.03	0.04	0.04
Not stated	–	–	0.14

Source: Compiled from the Census of India reports of 1991, 2001 and 2011.

The Table 2.1 exhibits that the proportion of the Muslim population is consistently increasing. Their proportion rises from 7.12 per cent in 1991 to 7.95 per cent in 2001 and 8.6 per cent in 2011 indicating towards migration since there is no trend of religious conversion from Hindus or any other religions to Muslims. Rather a proportional rise of Christians may be justified through conversion among the tribal people, from Hinduism to Christianity. Moreover, the government estimated about 325,400 illegal immigrants in Tripura (Parliament of India, 2014).

Theoretical Framework

Push and pull theory of migration is one of the most important theories, useful for listing the significant factors of migration. The theory is based on equilibrium and individual choice, so as to address the reasons or motivation behind migration. The push-pull theory is, however, a static model as it focuses on external factors of migration, which is unable to analyse the migration process as an integral part of broader transformation processes (Manju, 2013).

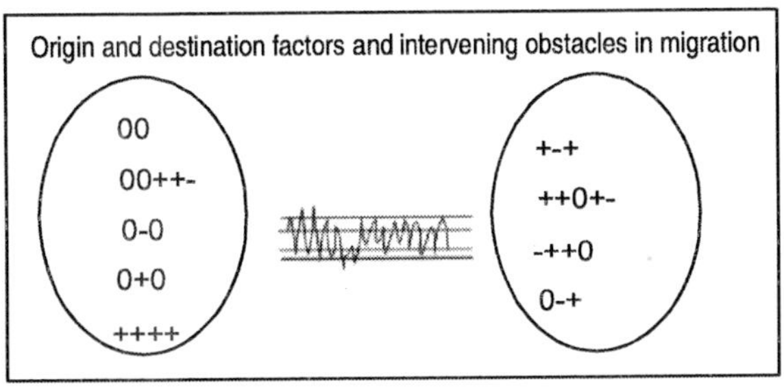

Fig. 2.1: Schematic of the push-pull model

To overcome the limitation, Lee developed the push-pull model in order to analyse the volume of migration, the characteristics of migrants and the factors which lead the migration decision-making process. According to him, push-pull factors are respectively repulsive and attractive forces. He portrayed push-pull factors into three broad sets of factors related to place of origin, destination and intervening obstacles (like cultural differences, distance, language differences and physical barrier, etc.) as perceived by individual migrants (Lee, 1966). Manju (2013) has categorised a few reasons, related to the origin, as push factors such as extreme poverty, unhealthy climate, political or religious suppression, life threat due to any other cause etc. On the other side, better employment opportunities, comfortable living, having natural resources like land or valuable minerals, social and religious freedom, in destination place are the pull factors. Both the push-pull factors work as a set of factors for the movement of people from one place to another (Eze, 2016).

Objective and Methodology

The specific objectives of the present study are: (a) to examine push-pull factors of migration from Bangladesh into Tripura; and (b) to understand the religious association of push-pull factors. The methodology adopted is quantitative. The study completely stands on primary data.

Sampling framework: Purposive snowball sampling procedure was followed for the selection of the sample. Keeping in view the ATTF Accord, immigrants (migrants from Bangladesh) were chosen for the study. Total of 128 samples were surveyed.

Study area: Sepahijala district, previously under undivided West Tripura district, has an area of 1043.04 sq. km. with a total population of 542,731 persons. The prime livelihood source is agriculture. The said district, located along the India-Bangladesh border, has been selected for the study. The district has witnessed a huge demographic change in terms of community. Moreover, the district has an open boundary with Bangladesh which may be conducive for the influx of people from across the border.

Analytical framework: After reviewing available literature a total of eight factors behind migration, in the form of multiple responses, was asked from the identified respondents. Their responses were calculated in percentage form. To deal with the first objective of the study, eight factors were analysed by Principal Component Analysis method in order to reduce all factors into smaller dimensions. Produced factor score of eight factors categorised in terms of their push-pull nature along with other socio-economic and political dimension. For a set of factors $X_1, X_2 \ldots\ldots, X_p$, principal components may be written as,

$$\begin{aligned} PC_1 &= a_{11}X_1 + a_{12}X_2 + \ldots + a_{1p}X_p \\ PC_2 &= a_{21}X_1 + a_{22}X_2 + \ldots + a_{2p}X_p \\ PC_p &= a_{p1}X_1 + a_{p2}X_2 + \ldots + a_{pp}X_p \end{aligned} \qquad \ldots (1)$$

Where a_{pp} represents the weight for the pth principal component and the pth variable. The coefficient of the first principal component $a_{11,}$ $a_{12,}$ $\ldots, a_{1p}$ are chosen in such a way that the variance of PC_1 is maximised subject to the condition that: $a_{11}^2 + a_{12}^2 + \ldots + a_{1p}^2 = 1$

The second principal component explains less variation in the original variable as compare to the first component subject to the above condition and they are completely uncorrelated. Similarly, the rests of the components also explain small and smaller variations in the original variable without any correlation with their previous components (Xhafaj, 2015). Binary Logistic Regression is applied to the composite factor score of principal components in order to understand the religious association of push-pull factors. The functional form of the binary logistic model may be written as equation 2,

$$Z_i = \ln \frac{P_i}{[1-p_i]} = \alpha + \beta X_{1i} + \gamma X_{2i} + \ldots + \delta X + \varepsilon_i \qquad \ldots (2)$$

Here, Zi is a log odds, α is constant, β, γ, δ are vectors of coefficients of independent variables (*see* Table 2.1), X_{1i}, X_{2i}, ..., Xni and ε_i is an error term for ith respondents. In the above equation, the only change in log odds of the dependent variable calculates by coefficients, not the change in the variable itself. Therefore, the logit equation may be converted into odds ratio by using the exponential function in order to make an easy interpretation. Now the functional form of odds ratio may be written as equation 3,

$$\text{Odds ratio} = \frac{P_i}{[1-p_i]} = e^{(\alpha + \beta X_{1i} + \gamma x_{2i} + \ldots + \delta x + \varepsilon_i)} \qquad \ldots (3)$$

Here, odds ratio means the ratio of the probability that a respondent will become Muslim by religion to the probability that the respondent will belong to the Hindu community. The sign of the coefficient of the composite factor indicates the direction of change.

Results and Discussions

The largest section of migrants belonged to the Muslim community with almost 59.4 per cent proportion, followed by 40.6 per cent Hindus. Expectedly, more than half of the respondents were male with 62.5 per cent proportion (*see* Table 2.2).

Table 2.2: Basic Profile of the Respondents

Religious distribution		*Gender distribution*	
Hindu	52 (40.6)	Male	80 (62.50)
Muslim	76 (59.4)	Female	48 (37.50)
Total	128 (100)	Total	128 (100)
Age distribution		**Educational qualification**	
Below 18	6 (4.69)	Illiterate	42 (32.8)
18-24	30 (23.44)	Literate (without formal education)	30 (23.4)
25-31	40 (31.25)	Primary	24 (18.8)
32-38	26 (20.31)	Upper Primary	14 (10.9)
39-45	16 (12.50)	Higher secondary	16 (12.5)
46 and above	10 (7.81)	Graduate and above	2 (1.6)
Total	128 (100)	Total	128 (100)

Source: Field survey, 2018; Parentheses indicate the percentage

Age distribution shows that prominent numbers of migrants belong to 25-31 years age group with almost 31.25 per cent proportion, followed by 18-24 years age group with 23 per cent proportion (*see* Table 2.2). This indicates the largest sections of migrants are young who left origin country. Small factions of migrants belong to 46 and above age group. Only six migrants, below 18 years age, were interviewed (*see* Table 2.2). Above this, one migrant was found to be child labour. Expectedly, prominent sections of migrants are found illiterate with 32.8 per cent proportion, followed by normal literates (without formal education) with 23 per cent proportion. More than half of migrants reported having no schooling as compared to almost 29 per cent of migrants having elementary (primary + upper primary) level of education (*see* Table 2.2). A small proportion of migrants reported having a higher secondary degree and only two migrants found to have graduation degree from Bangladesh.

Push-Pull Factors

Total 82 migrants, almost 64.1 per cent of all, identified 'lack of employment opportunity in Bangladesh' as one of the important factors behind their migration. Overall, this factor emerged as the most popular reason with 16.6 per cent proportion out of all reasons. The ethnic and cultural links have been reported by almost 62.5 per cent migrants as the reason of migration and that reason was found as a second prominent factor with 16.2 per cent proportion out of all responses (*see* Table 2.3).

Table 2.3: Reasons for Migrating from Bangladesh to Tripura

	*Responses**		*Percentage based on answers (%)**
	N	*Percentage based on respondents (%)*	
Lack of employment opportunity in Bangladesh	82	64.1	16.6
Stronger value of Indian currency	68	53.1	13.8
Poverty in Bangladesh	58	45.3	11.7
Forced grabbing of landed property	62	48.4	12.6
Religious persecution	50	39.1	10.1
Cultural or ethnic similarity in Tripura	80	62.5	16.2
Political welcome in India	58	45.3	11.7
Marriage	36	28.1	7.3
Total	128	100.0	100.0

Source: Field survey, 2018. *Calculated by authors

More than half of migrants, almost 53 per cent reported that 'stronger value of Indian currency as compared to Bangladesh' attracted them to settle down in India. The reason got 13 per cent selection out of all surveyed reasons (*see* Table 2.3). Almost 48.4 per cent of migrants reported incidents of forced land grabbing as the reason for leaving Bangladesh. There is a controversial legislation in Bangladesh called the Vested Property Act, earlier known as the Enemy Property Act of 1965. There are hardly any minority households in Bangladesh that had not lost their properties under this infamous law. Abusing this law, the government had already seized almost three million acres of Hindu land and leased them to Muslims (Guha, 2010).

Almost 39.1 per cent of respondents reported that they had to leave Bangladesh because of religious persecution. The extent of religious persecution over religious minorities (especially on Hindus) can be assessed by their abnormal reduction in Bangladesh population. The Hindu population has consistently declined in Bangladesh. During 1961, the proportion of Hindu Bengali was 18 per cent in erstwhile East Bengal and according to the last census report in 2011, the proportion of Hindu Bengali was recorded only about 8 per cent in the country.[1] According to a Bangladeshi daily, as quoted by a human rights activist in a speech during 55th session of the sub-commission on the Promotion and Protection of Human Rights (United Nations, July 28-August 15, 2003) in Geneva, "Within the first 92 days since the election was held, 80 were killed, 2,811 injured and 228 women were raped by the members and supporters of the BNP (Bangladesh Nationalist Party). 225 out of the raped women belong to the minority communities, whose age range from 8 to 50" (Haralaka, 2008).

Both the reasons, political welcome in India and poverty in Bangladesh, were reported by almost 45 per cent migrants and simultaneously these two reasons included almost 23 per cent proportion of all answers (*see* Table 2.3). The matrimonial alliance is witnessed as the least popular reason, reported by only 28 per cent of migrants, behind migration from Bangladesh in the study area. The reason marriage, behind migration, counted only seven per cent responses out of all. During the field study, it was found that a lot of respondents (both male and female) have entered India only for marriage and settled down over there (*see* Table 2.3).

Before running PCA all variables have gone through Kaiser-Meyer-Olkin Measure (KMO) of Sampling Adequacy. The result shows that PCA can be done as the value is 0.499, which is very close to 0.5. Total of eight factors for migration have been included for principal component analysis. They explained total of 70.17 per cent variation (*see* Table 2.4). As usual, the first factor explains the highest variance (27.85 per cent), followed by the second factor with 24.41 per cent of the total variation. Similarly, the third factor reveals 17.91 per cent variation.

***First factor*:** The factor includes total of three reasons behind migration with a few notable points. This consists of 'lack of employment opportunity in Bangladesh', 'forced grabbing of landed property' and 'religious persecution'. The factor reveals that all the reasons indicate induced migration. This means that these have to be considered as push factors. However, from a sociological perspective, these reasons may not take place in the same bracket. A migrant, who left Bangladesh due to lack of employment opportunities, is undoubtedly an economic migrant. Those migrants had to flee away from their origin country due to land grabbing and religious persecutions, they may be considered a refugee or asylum seeker. Despite having the categorical difference between economic migrant and asylum seeker, the respondents, who reported about these reasons behind migration, are forced migrants as because they were bound to migrate either due to economic depression or any socio-political aggression. Therefore, it can be assumed that the first factor included significant push factors in the same bracket.

Table 2.4: Results of PCA

	Factors			*Domain*
	1	2	3	
Lack of employment opportunity in Bangladesh	**-.572**	-.113	.455	Economic
Stronger value of Indian currency	-.109	-.146	**.813**	Economic
Poverty in Bangladesh	-.108	-.242	**-.768**	Economic
Forced grabbing of landed property	**.937**	-.057	.095	Political
Religious persecution	**.930**	.003	-.011	Social
Ethnic or cultural similarity	-.079	**.824**	.080	Social
Political welcome in India	-.109	**-.769**	.166	Political
Marriage	-.033	**.633**	.484	Social
Variance (%)	**27.85**	**24.41**	**17.91**	**Total (70.17)**
Extraction Method	Principal Component Analysis.			
Rotation method	Varimax with Kaiser Normalisation.			
KMO Measure	0.499			

The result indicates push factors have a different direction towards migration. The factor loading of the reason "Lack of employment opportunity" has come up with a negative sign. It indicates employment opportunity has an inverse relationship with migration. In other words, as much as employment opportunity decreases in Bangladesh, the influx towards India as well as Tripura increases. Again, "forced grabbing of landed property" and "religious persecution" are positively associated with migration. It is a clear indication that migration increases due to these reasons in the direct proportional way.

***Second factor*:** The second factor includes three reasons 'ethnic or cultural similarity', 'political welcome in India' and 'marriage'. It may assume that these three reasons have been paired up in the same bracket as the pull factors. At present, almost 70 per cent people of Tripura are Bengali across the religion and especially border areas of the state are dominated by the Muslims. Therefore, the ethnic similarity made easier to get access to local communities for Bangladeshi immigrants. Moreover, the similarity of language is also an advantage for the immigrants. Due to this homogeneity, it becomes tough to single out any immigrant. Marriage is nothing but a supplementary of ethnic links. Bangladeshi girls prefer Indian youth not only because of ethnic links but also for better economic security in India as well as in Tripura. Literally, Bangladeshi immigrants are being cordially welcomed by the politicians from the very beginning. Bangladeshi immigrants are always popular as loyal and organised vote-bank among political parties in Tripura as because they will never be able to betray to that leader or party, due to whom he or she got access into Indian periphery with all official documents.

However, the result indicating the direction of all pull factors are not the same. The factor score of ethnic similarity is positive, which indicates the directly proportional relationship with migration. This means that strong higher loading of 'ethnic similarity' directly works as a catalyst for migration. Similarly, the positive factor loading of the reason 'marriage' indicates the large scale of migration. Interestingly, 'political welcome in India' has a negative but strong factor loading. This negative sign of that reason is indicating that always migration does not increase with political welcome. The justification may be considered as always Hindu immigrants are not politically accepted into the host country as compared to their Muslim counterparts (Fig. 2.2).

***Third factor*:** This factor includes two economic reasons namely, 'stronger value of Indian currency' and 'poverty in Bangladesh', in the same dimension with a different direction. Categorically, the former represents pull factor and the latter represents push factor. Despite having

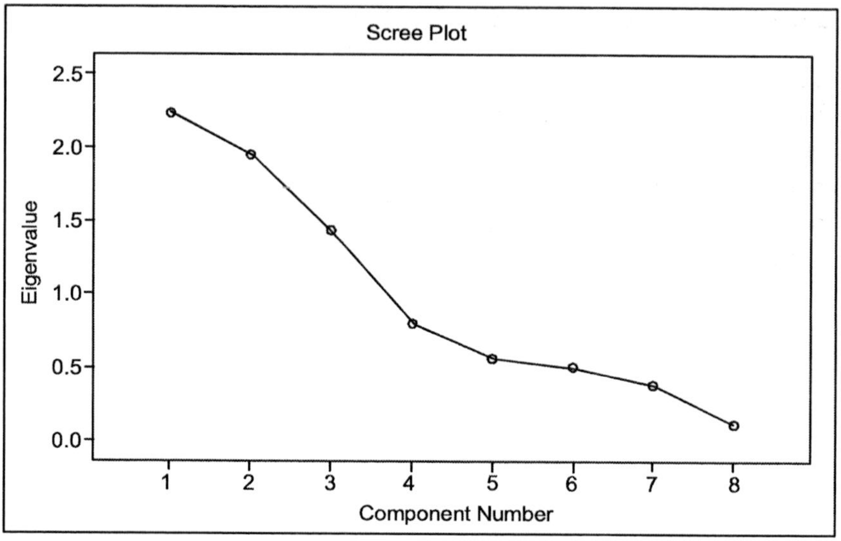

Fig. 2.2: Scree plot

heterogeneity in terms of push and pull factors, both represent economic reasons behind migration within the same bracket. Expectedly, the stronger value of Indian currency attracted Bangladeshi immigrants as the Indian currency is profitable to them in the form of remittance into their origin country. Poverty, undoubtedly, compels citizens of underdeveloped countries to migrate into the developing or developed countries.

The positive factor score of the reason 'stronger value of Indian currency' is clearly indicating a directly proportional relationship with migration as a pull factor. The probability of a Bangladeshi citizen to migrate into India as well as Tripura increases with increasing value of Indian currency as compared to Bangladesh. The negative but strong factor score indicates that if poverty increases in Bangladesh, it does not always influence migration. Few justifications may be considered like Bangladeshi immigrants, mainly semi-skilled or unskilled labour, enter India for the comparatively better livelihoods. They are popular in the labour market of Tripura as because of the willingness to work with a low wage rate. Therefore, the earnings from India as well as Tripura meet only a few basic necessities of Bangladeshi immigrants rather than upgrading their economic status. This may be the fact that poverty does not always induce Bangladeshi nationals to migrate into Tripura.

Religious Association of Push-Pull Factors

The composite score of the factors was regressed on the religion of Bangladeshi immigrants since the value (0.64) of R square indicates the good fitness of the model. Table 2.5 shows that only Factor-1 has a significant relationship with the religion of Bangladeshi immigrants in Tripura. Rest two factors have no significant association with the same. The Factor-1 is negatively associated with the odds of the religion of Bangladeshi immigrants. That means the likelihood of a Bangladeshi immigrant to be Hindu is significantly higher for these reasons loaded in Factor-1.

Table 2.5: Binary Logistic Model

Dependent variable		*Religion of immigrant (Muslim/Hindu)*		
Variables	*B*	*Std. Error*	*p-value*	*Exp. (B)*
Constant	0.693	0.287	0.016	1.999
Factor-1	-2.152	0.371	0.000***	0.116
Factor-2	-.139	0.290	0.632	0.871
Factor-3	-.030	0.259	0.907	0.970
Nagelkerke R Square			0.64	

****Significant at 1% level.*

Now, Factor-1 includes 'lack of employment opportunity in Bangladesh', 'forced grabbing of landed property' and 'religious persecution'. The above binary logistic model reveals that if an immigrant reported to those reasons behind his or her migration, the probability of being Hindu of that immigrant is higher. Few separate grounds may be considered as justification for each reason in regard to the religion of immigrants. Since Bangladesh has been declared as an Islamic country, it is crystal clear that employment opportunities for the religious minorities, i.e. for the Hindu Bangladeshi citizens, are limited as compared to their majority counterparts. This means that the influx of Hindu immigrants is highly influenced by inadequate employment opportunities in Bangladesh as compared to their majority counterparts. The eviction of Hindu families from their ancestral property is a common phenomenon in Bangladesh. The Enemy Property Act, however, did not encourage encroachment of Hindu property rights rather it is being misused by the radical political activists. Similarly, religious persecution of the Hindus in Bangladesh is a matter of deep concern.

Rest of the factors does not significantly determine the religion of immigrants. Factor-2 includes ethnic similarity, marriage and political welcome. These reasons have no religious obligation. Suppose, ethnic similarity itself indicating about Bengali homogeneity rather than the religion of a Bengali and similarly marriage is also a supplementary part of ethnic similarity. Factor-3 includes strong Indian currency value and poverty in Bangladesh; both are economic reasons, therefore, an economic immigrant may belong to any community. Therefore, if an immigrant prefers any of these reasons before leaving the origin country, religion does not matter.

Concluding Remarks

Both push and pull factors are responsible behind Bangladeshi migration into Tripura. The limited employment opportunities in Bangladesh have been witnessed as the most popular push factor and ethnic similarity in Tripura as the most prominent pull factor behind migration. Beyond the nature of reason (either economic or socio-political), reporting any of the push factors by any immigrant indicates that by force he or she had to leave the origin country. However, the reason 'better employment opportunity in the destination (Tripura)' can also be considered as pull factor rather than push factor. A large section of Bangladeshi agricultural labourers and construction workers are hired by local contractors in Tripura as seasonal migrants. Due to a few special characteristics and extraordinary working approach, they are very popular than the native workers in the labour market. Bangladeshi labourers are always willing to work with low wage rate and they never go for any bargaining. Literally, they used to work at least ten hours a day. Moreover, always seasonal migrants are used to joining into any work with a mission mode so that they can return back to their home within a particular timeframe after finishing the assignment. Therefore, sometimes sky touching demand for Bangladeshi cheap labour becomes more influential factor than lack of employment opportunity into their homeland. On another hand, the same factor, the lack of employment opportunities becomes push factor for Bangladeshi Hindus or the religious minorities. They had to face communal discrimination in terms of getting employment opportunities. In this case, the factor definitely worked as a push factor for the religious minorities of Bangladesh. Interestingly as far as the religion of immigrants is a concern, only push factors of migration to have a religious association and whatever the domain (economic or socio-political) may be. Push factors like lack of employment opportunities in Bangladesh, forced grabbing of landed property and religious persecution are directly associated with the religion of immigrants. According to the above analysed binary model, these three reasons determine the religion of a Bangladeshi immigrant. Although the lack of employment opportunity is a common problem in Bangladesh, yet Hindu Bangladeshi nationals are being suppressed at the workplace just because of their religion. Besides, land grabbing cases and religious persecution are definitely subject to the migration of Hindus. In other words, pull factors significantly do not determine the religion of a Bangladeshi migrant in Tripura. For instance, cultural or ethnic similarity has no relationship with the religion as all migrants are Bengalis. Similarly, other economic reasons like poverty in Bangladesh and stronger value of Indian currency are undoubtedly always equal across all the communities. Therefore, pull factors equally affect the decision of migration process across both religions. In other words, pull factors do not have any relationship with the religion of Bangladeshi immigrants of Tripura.

Note

1. Census Reports (1941-2011), East Pakistan and Bangladesh.

References

ATTF Accord, 1993. *Memorandum of Settlement: Tripura State Government and ATTF Accord.* Online available at https://www.ucdp.uu.se/downloads/ fullpeace/ IND%2019930823.pdf (Accessed on December 4, 2017).

Bhattacharyya, Gayatri, 1988. *Refugee Rehabilitation and Its Impact on Tripura's Economy*, New Delhi: Omsons Publications.

Bhaumik, Subir, 2012. 'Tripura: Ethnic Conflict, Militancy and Counterinsurgency', *Policies and Practices 52*, Kolkata: Mahanirban Calcutta Research Group.

Deb, M.K., &Mahato, A., 2017. 'Understanding the Politics around Illegal Migration from Bangladesh into Assam and Tripura', *Asian Journal of Research in Social Sciences and Humanities*, 7(9), 222-234.

De, Nilanjan, 2013. 'Migration and Its Terminological Variation in Tripura: An analytical study', *Asian Journal of Research in Social Sciences and Humanities*, 3(11).

Eze, Basil U., 2016. 'The Underlying Factors of Rural-Urban Migration in South-eastern Nigeria: A Study in Nsukka Region of Enugu State', *IOSR Journal of Humanities and Social Science*, 21(7), 46-54.

Gordon, M., 1998. *Dictionary of Sociology*. New York: Oxford.

Guha, S., 2010. 'Bangladesh Enemy Property Act: 1965-2010: How long must we bear this burden?',

Online available at http://www.vijayvaani.com/ArticleDisplay.aspx?aid=1498 (Accessed on September 20, 2017).

Haralaka, S., 2008. *Bangladeshi Invasion*, Guwahati: Self Published.

Lee, Everett S., 1966. 'A Theory of Migration', *Demography*, 3(1), 47-57.

Mahato, A. & Deb, M.K., 2017. 'Understanding Tipraland Movement through Migration in Tripura', *Indian Journal of Social Research*, 58(6), 823-837.

Manju, 2013. *Patterns of internal migration and its correlates in India during the 1990s*, Unpublished PhD thesis. Rohtak: Department of Geography, Maharshi Dayanand University.

Parliament of India, 2014. Answer to Rajya Sabha Unstarred Question No. 332, New Delhi.

Xhafaj, E., 2015. 'The Principal Components Analysis and Cluster Analysis as Tools for the Estimation of Poverty: An Albanian Case Study', *International Journal of Science and Research*, 4(1), 1240-43.

3

The People of Nowhere

Narratives of Bengali Settlers in Shillong

Anamika Deb Roy

The forces of globalisation have led people to believe that in the world now, there exists but one unified culture. However, on the other hand, various political assertions emphasise an insular, local cultural and ethnic difference which has gone on to be loudly advocated for and asserted in many parts of the world. Such is the case in the state of Meghalaya too, where the dominant ethnic group in the region, especially those who derive their legitimacy from the agency of indigeneity, have gone on to loudly voice their difference from those whom they perceive as the 'others', 'outsider' or 'settler'. The Bengalis form a large section of the so-called 'others' in the state of Meghalaya, and since their migration to the state till the present day often are faced with the dilemma of who they are and what their identity is in the place they call home.

The contemporary world is confronted with an ironic condition where, on the one hand, there is an increasing standardisation of cultural values aided by the forces of globalisation that often lead people to believe that there now exists one unified culture, while on the other hand, political assertions emphasise an insular, local cultural and ethnic difference which has gone on to be loudly advocated for and asserted in many parts of the world. Such is the case in Northeast India too, where almost every ethnic group in the region, especially those who derive their legitimacy from the agency of indigeneity is engaged in the act of narrativising a glorious past that is fashioned in a manner to valourise their difference from 'others'. In the state of Meghalaya which has a major tribal population, the 'others' comprise of a group of non-tribal people comprising of the Assamese, Bengalis, Nepalis, Marwaris, Sindhis and small sections of communities from many different parts of the country. This paper proposes to identify the existential dilemmas of the 'settler Bengali' community in the state who appear to be caught at the intersection of the tremors of the trials and tribulations of the partition of India that saw their ancestors migrated from their native homelands to a new land which gave them a new identity with the partition and at the same time, they now experience the travails of an invisible partition in the social and political clime of the region they live in which demarcates them forever as the 'other', 'outsider' or 'settler'.

Locating the Bengalis in Shillong

To better understand the arrival of the Bengalis to the then province of Assam, one would have to go down further in history when Sylhet was part and parcel of the same unfractured and undivided region. As David Ludden observes "When the traveller Ibn Batuta met Shah Jalal, in 1346, the Sylhet landscape held diverse territories of Khasis, Garos, Hindus, Muslims and others" (2003, 51). Sylhet became part of the Mughal Empire and emerged as a frontier town of its Bengal Suba (province) in 1612. With the British East India Company acquiring Diwani of Bengal in 1765, the region came under its administration, and the adjoining regions of Assam and Cachar were annexed to British territory respectively in 1826 and 1832. Out of the 'unwieldy' Bengal Presidency, some districts from Assam were separated and clubbed with Cachar, Goalpara, Garo Hills and the other hill districts to create a new Chief Commissioner's province in 1874. However, as a new province with inadequate revenue potential Assam could hardly take up the responsibility of governance. "To make it financially viable, the authorities, therefore, decided in September to incorporate into it the populous, Bengali-speaking district of Sylhet which historically as well as ethnically, was an integral part of Bengal" (Guha 1977, 27).

The 'settler' Bengalis arrived in the state of Meghalaya (previously part of the undivided Assam) alongside the British administration sometime between 1863 and 1866 much before the official inclusion of Sylhet in the Chief Commissioner's province. Records, in fact, reveal that it was in 1863 that an entrepreneur from Sylhet called Ghulam Hyder first migrated to Cherrapunjee and later settled in Shillong when the British made it a station. In 1866, Krishna Kishore Dhar, a British government official along with 27 other Bengalis settled in the Shillong station aiding the government officials in carrying out their day-to-day business. The history of the early Bengali 'settlement' thus reveals that the 'first' Bengalis arrived not only at a period when historical claims to space were justified for the colonisers, but when requirements of a colonial administration provided opportunities only to the emerging educated sections. Therefore, the 'indigenous' communities who had not yet made acquaintance with modern western education were obviously confined to the margins of the social and political settings.

The narratives evoking this past history, reveal no sense of any adversarial discord between the 'settler' community and the 'indigenous' community, and rather, on the contrary, exhibits an era of shared experiences that was buttressed by trade and friendship in a common cultural space. A major factor that could have possibly led to this is that both the settlers and the indigenous people had a common adversary — the British, and as such a narration about that period depicts mutually desired and cooperative interactions between the settler and the indigenous members. Contributions of people like Nilmoni Chakraborty who had gone on to collate the resistance of the Khasis in the Shella region against the construction of a dam as well as against the collection of contributions for the famine affected people in the area in 1901 are some of the best examples of a period of peaceful coexistence. His assistance to the people of Mawlong in recovering land from the Chatak English Company is yet another instance of the mutually gratifying interaction between the two communities. These 'accommodative relations', as Robin Williams (1964:17) explains in a different context, possibly rested upon an 'economic interdependence that (was) mutually advantageous and essentially non-competitive'. The existence of such a shared space was visible in other areas of interaction as well. Members of the settler community were quite proficient at using the local language in addition to having knowledge of English, and it is a common known fact that a Bengali named Krishna Chandra Pal in 1813 provided the Khasis with a script. It was, in fact, another Bengali, Ashutosh Mukherjee, the Vice Chancellor of Calcutta University, who granted recognition to Khasi as a language of examination for matriculation. These historical facts make it clear that till a certain point of time, members from the ethnic dominant groups' revealed nonchalance for any ethnic hierarchy.

The question which then arises is, if there was such a past where peaceful cohabitation had been the norm, what could have led to the adversarial attitude that members of both communities have come to hold against each other which has led to a lack of trust between the ethnic groups leading to a fracture in an erstwhile peaceful society.

The answer to this question can be possibly found in the trajectory pursued by the new state's justification for the creation of a state separate from Assam. Meghalaya was created in deference to claims for ethnic autonomy and, for some scholars, electoral remunerations, and on both the accounts it was necessary for the new state to pursue a political and social strategy that consolidated and nurtured claims along ethnic outlines. This outcome appears logical and even justifiable if we consider how group autonomy and representation is recognised and negotiated along ethnic distinctions in India's Northeast. Notably, in this region, ethnic claims have also often been squared by recognising ethnicity as not only the foundation of the social and political constituency and the axis of political and social mobilisation but also the conscious and unconscious creation of an asymmetry between 'indigenous' and 'national' norms. This asymmetry results primarily because "the (cultural) autonomy they seek preserves customary law and practices, which imply unequal rights or discrimination against outsiders as well as insiders" (Ghai 2000, 7) leading to the inevitable marginalisation of 'others'. The conception of Meghalaya was also made on this principle and thus, the 'indigenous' dominant groups are viewed as the "centre of everything, and all others are scaled and rated with reference to it" (Williams 1964, 39).

If one were to view the narratives of the settler community on the basis of a timeframe and understand the sense of self-identity of the community over different points of time, it becomes clear that while these narratives during the British period helped conjure a positive and assertive sense of self-identity, in contemporary times it conjures a defeatist and victimised sense of self-identity for the community. This is probably because from being a socially dominant minority, after the formation of Meghalaya, the settlers have been forced to go on a back foot and experience a massive sense of loss. They are no longer considered historical subjects who provide content to the crafting of a specific image and history of the state, but rather all contributions of the settlers are considered as differing and competing with the indigenous history necessary to legitimise the uniqueness claim of the dominant majority. In the new state where the content and character of ethnic identity determines social and political privileges, the settlers were 'otherised' through the enactment of legal restrictions and production of social images that contests their legitimacy as equal members of the new society.

In chronicling the contributions and role of individuals and members of the community and evaluating their relative importance under the changing historical context, the community not only seeks to rediscover and redefine its past but also makes an effort to express the contemporary crisis of ethnic legitimisation. These chronicles go on to highlight the predicament of a 'nowhere' people who are engaged in the act of recovering a luminous history in a futile attempt to alter the disadvantages of the present. It would be pertinent to note here that in individualising their history the settler community makes an attempt to rise above their present crisis by disassociating themselves with the second phase of settlers who came as victims of a bloody partition. Thus, as original migrants and settlers in a place where they came by choice and not because they had no other choice, they claim to be part of the state that now refuses to acknowledge its existence with equal rights. The moral justification goes on to reveal the internal contradictions prevalent in a community that fails to comprehend its contemporary subject position in the state where they are always the outsider or 'dkhar' but also reflects on their fractured sense of identity as a community at large.

The community which had experienced the tremors and travails of a 'visible partition' almost two generations earlier, is now experiencing the travails of an 'invisible partition' that sees them as socially and politically projected as the other/settler/outsider. The commitments made to these settlers by the tribal leaders whose commitment to live according to their own genius led to the creation of the state, are often perceived to be have been reneged soon when concerns for the ethnic homogeneity and exclusive rights of the indigenous groups became the adopted political idiom. The settlers who basically came in two phases: one group before the partition as landowners or agents of the British government and the other as victims of a gory partition have come to be represented as the adversarial other within the new state. Dominant representations not only place them at the lowest rung in the ladder of social and political hierarchy and perpetuate social images of them as the occupants and outsiders as common terms like 'dkhar' and 'kharbang' would indicate but also excludes them from being narrators and actors of the new history of the state.

Ethos in Literature

By 1947, outward hegemony had been supplanted by inward hegemony, in the form of the Indian state. The setting up of the autonomous district council in 1952 triggered the formation of the 'hill state' movement, while the demand by the Assam Provincial Congress Committee, to make Assamese the official language in 1960, acted as a catalyst to this. Hegemony was made manifest not only in the attempt to impose a language but was made concrete and visible through the acquisition of land. This led to riots against the Assamese in the 1960s. The dominant discourse of identity politics had already been set on the construction of the 'other'. With the onset of globalisation, the need to reformulate identity and self-representation became necessary. When the British left, mobilisation along the lines of ethnic identity was not as powerful as during the period after India's independence which saw the emergence of the middle-class in full-blown proportion. This new middle-class played a crucial role in the political arena. The period between 1946 and 1970 saw the formation of various regional organisations like the Khasi National Durbar in the early 1920s and regional political organisations such as the Khasi Hills People's Union (KHPU), All Party Hills Leaders Conference (APHLC) and the Hills States People's Democratic Party (HSPDP). An idea of ethnic identity or rather the construct of ethnic identity became the basis of what was to gradually develop and to be made concrete into the form of the state of Meghalaya in 1972. Post-1972 however, there was a growing realisation that it is not enough to be politically represented and that control of the cultural space was necessary. Mobilisation along communal lines had gained momentum. This was made evident through the various riots of the 1960s, 1970s and 1980s against the Assamese, Bengalis and Nepalis respectively, and the emergence of the Khasi Students Union (KSU) in 1978, which aimed at upholding Khasi identity and fighting against the infiltration of outsiders. The KSU went on to hold a sway over the people; in addition to the former it openly opposed and criticised the more militant Hynniewtrep National Liberation Council (HNLC) in the coming years for its militant outlook towards Garos and the so-called outsiders.

It is thus but natural that writers writing in the late twentieth and early twenty-first century should reflect on the turmoil and unrest of the times in their works. Two writers in recent times whose books on this crucial question of identity that has gone on to grab much attention are Anjum Hasan's *Lunatic in My Head* (2007) and Janice Pariat's *Boats on Land* (2012). Hailing from Shillong, both writers in their texts attempt to grapple with the question 'Who is an actual native of the state?' One who belongs to the tribe, or also one who is born and brought up in the city, though essentially not of the hills, but for whom there is no place called home but these hills. What does it mean to be a Khasi and a non-Khasi in a state torn by identity politics? Does being a native of the state refer to only to the Khasi identity or does it also include those who perhaps do not belong to the tribal groups inhabiting the state, but who nonetheless feel like they belong to the state, and are thus not outsiders having been raised in the place that has gone on to determine the very way they lead their lives? These are some of the questions that both Hasan and Pariat go on to raise in their texts.

A common term used to address the outsider, one who can trace the roots of his or her ancestry back to the plains in Shillong is 'dkhar', and this is a condescending term by all means. The natives view these people as outsiders who are nothing but a threat to the opportunities and development of the hill people, thus creating a mindset of a need to eliminate their threatening presence from the state. However, having been born and raised in the place they have always called home, these 'outsiders' have no other home but these hills and are left baffled and bewildered at the sudden claims of what they always supposed to have been their home as something that was never theirs to claim as their own in the very first place. Such is the case of the Bengalis too who, as has been mentioned earlier, migrated to Meghalaya and went on to own land and jobs and play an active role in the civil society, till their such claims came to be challenged at a later date.

Both Hasan and Pariat base their books along these lines of identity politics that is rife in the state of Meghalaya. Titled after the lyrics of the band Pink Floyd's famous song *Brain Damage*, Hasan's novel like Floyd's song has for its protagonist people who are misfits, and are regarded as weird at times for not conforming to the strict rules of society, where society is a complex system in which people are conditioned to behave in a certain way. The three protagonists of the book Firdaus Ansari, Aman Moondy, and Sophie Das are thus all misfits and have a lunatic raging in their head constantly making them doubt their position in a universe where everyone else appears to be sure of their position in the larger scheme of things, whereas they, on the other hand, are constantly confounded with notions of who they are. It is thus that Firdaus Ansari;

> ... refused to introduce herself as a Bihari because though her parents were from Bihar, she was born in Shillong and had never lived anywhere else. What did that make her? In Shillong's eyes if

> nothing else at least a dkhar, a foreigner, someone who did not have roots here, did not have the ground needed to put roots in (Hasan 2007, 4).

Aman Moondy when confronted with the sole choice of being sent to Delhi by his father Dr. Moondy to determine his future career choices on having failed the Civil Services examination for the second time desperately thought, "I can't go" (Hasan 2007, 331), for him Shillong is the only place he belongs to. And for eight year old Sophie Das, a young Bengali girl who is stuck with insensitive parents who neither understand nor try to understand the longings of this hyper-imaginative eight year old, "the nicest thing, the nicest thing by far, even better than being adopted, would be if she could somehow turn into one of them, somehow become Khasi" (Hasan 2007, 99). At every turn, these characters' claims of what should have always been their home, as something that was never theirs to claim as their own in the very first place, is contested upon. It is a place where "people were afraid of each other ... dkhars were afraid of tribals, tribals were afraid of dkhars" (Hasan 2007, 72).

Anjum Hasan in an interview to *The Hindu* on January 6, 2008, says, "I don't want to get into the politics of it, but there has always been an invisible line between the insiders and the outsiders in Shillong."[1] This she feels is inevitable. It is culturally very distinct. And then, most outsiders who settled down in Shillong were either handling trade or holding government jobs. In small towns, with little opportunities, these things matter.

Published in the year 2012, Janice Pariat's collection of short stories *Boats on Land* deals with this issue of identity in almost all her stories. In naming her anthology *Boats on Land*, Pariat sets the tone of all her tales. Pariat's stories grapple with the real and the unreal, the actual and the surreal. Just as a boat on land has no identity, and finds meaning only when it sets sail, the characters in Pariat's stories struggle with notions of home, identity and belonging.

Almost all of Pariat's stories reveal the disdain of the natives for the 'outsiders', be it the 'bilati' men during the British Raj in *A Waterfall of Horses*, or that of the 'dkhar', or people not hailing from the hills in *Secret Corridors*, *19/87*, *Laitlum* and almost all the other tales. Anyone who does not hail from the hills and whose ancestry cannot be traced back to the hills is forever viewed with suspicion by the natives. This is however not a recent phenomenon as many of us have been led to believe in the past that

Pariatreveals through the course of her stories. In *A Waterfall of Horses*, the villagers are unhappy with the presence of the 'bilati' men in their village. A question often asked is "When are they going to leave?" (Pariat 2012, 8). As the influx of the outsiders continues, the natives view them as objects of great dislike and often comment as Doreen does in *Secret Corridors* that the only solution to this problem is 'we need to kick them all out of our state' (Pariat 2012, 85). Anyone whose ancestry is not that of a Khasi is viewed with disdain and one is victimised in subtle ways for being a non-Khasi. Carmel, a girl of mixed ancestry whose mother is a single parent in the story *Secret Corridors*, is perhaps the best example of this state of victimhood. Pariat writes, "Within this classroom, like every other, there were invisible lines of demarcation as in any church or temple. Who it was acceptable to eat lunch with, who you could partner for arts and craft, who to include in your team for Danish rounders, and rising singularly above the rest, who you sat next to in class" (Pariat 2012, 82-83). *19/87*, a story set in the year 1987, a troubled year in the city of Shillong, torn apart by riots between the Khasis and the Nepalis, sees people comment anxiously, "it was the Nepalis in '79, the Bengalis in '81, then the Marwaris... who knows when it'll be our turn. We are what they call dkhars too" (Pariat 2012, 99).

In a city hostile towards the outsiders, both friendships and love affairs of people belonging to the two factions are subject to much disapproval, for the fear of the repercussions that such actions may have. It is thus that Natalie sits uncomfortably with her school friends when they pass foul comments about the non-tribal people, even though, "Her friends in the neighbourhood where she lived, whom she played with in the evenings, were Assamese. Like her, born and brought up here, and who considered Shillong their home" (Pariat 2012, 85), for fear of being called an "ieid-dkhar" or a dkhar lover, a condescending term at best. The love affair between a high school going young Barisha and her Assamese boyfriend, Vivek Hazarika is frowned upon by her family not because they disapprove of Vivek, but for the mere reason that having a non-tribal boyfriend will leave Barisha vulnerable to the hatred attacks of the fanatic 'tribal' faction of the society.

The contemporary society in Meghalaya is one that is confronted with an ironic condition, where on the one hand, increasing standardisation of cultural values released by forces of globalisation perceivably integrate everyone and lead many to believe that there is now but one culture. On the other hand, political assertions that emphasise an insular, local cultural difference and ethnic autonomy are acquiring ascendant legitimacy and articulation. The tribal people are thus engaged in the activity of recovery of the past that invalidates alleged hegemonic representations and in turn empowers the collectivity with a purported identity which is essentially self-referential. In this atmosphere of optimism and scepticism about the emergence of a global culture and an increasing deployment of cultural consciousness among specific groups, identities are constantly being fashioned and refashioned in a manner that is often depleted of the very symbolic resources necessary for their own ideological authority. In other words, the interaction of globalisation processes with local traditional culture has fashioned a new form of hybridisation that does not follow the linear perspectives of traditional and modern. In such an environment the notion of the identity of 'who is an actual native of the state' stands challenged.

Tussles between the traditional Khasis who follow the ancient animist religion, the new elite intelligentsia determined to forge a new identity based on the tenets of Christianity and western education, and the so-called 'outsider' who has gone on to settle in the hills thereby cutting off all ties with his ancestry that can be traced back outside the hills to set his roots firmly in the hills is unavoidable. It is for this very reason, that cultural identity has obtained political and economic values and inspires a need for the continual reinvention of tradition and cultural pasts. This activation of traditionalism may nevertheless aid the production and recovery of a form of historical consciousness, which culturally may be dispossessed of meaning, but is nevertheless an important political tool which undeniably assures benefits of participation. The ethnic Khasi groups thus go on to produce images of 'otherness', whereby the ethnic boundaries are politicised in an insular fashion that orchestrates and amplifies political conflicts. In pursuing this production of 'otherness', particular identities liberate a form of cultural politics that interweaves modern codes with traditional forms. It is thus that the question of 'who is an actual native?' becomes one of great significance.

Narratives, aural, oral and written have a foundational role in the construction of group identity or community and form an essential part of collective organisation and behaviour. As such narratives provide us with essential insights into not only the creative genius of a group but also furnish us with a repertoire of subjective experiences of that group.

India's Northeast, rich in its oral tradition of narration, is forced to reassess their tradition when confronted with the transformations set into motion with the onset of the forces of globalisation. As Rajesh Dev (2006, 80) in his essay *Narratives Claims and Identity Impasse* correctly observes,

> ... The encounter between global processes and discourses with embedded life-forms in a region of concentrated ethnic heterogeneity have released a form of 'collective determinism' that operates on very strict and complex principles of inclusion and exclusion operated through the contesting concept of 'indigeneity'.

It is thus that almost every ethnic community in this region in an attempt to derive a legitimacy of their existence is engaged in a process of narrativising their rich past in a fashion that both points out and revels in their difference from the 'others' and proceeds to grant a political recognition to this difference. The urge to enunciate an authentic collective identity by these groups makes them vehemently emphasise the certain arbitrary rule of selectivity that goes on to form a separate distinct identity not merged into the identity of the larger whole.

Most of the state structures in the Northeast region validate this issue of 'indigeneity' that goes on to give rise to the 'insider-outsider' politics within the social and political realms. The politics of representation pursued by the institutions of the state and dominant ethnic groups have gone on to reinforce and consolidate the exclusive meanings and subjective experiences of the communities around the ethnic state and ethnically demarcated territories. As such territories have proceeded to acquire fixed ethnic connotations that have in turn gone on to justify the claims of one being an 'insider'. The resulting lack of cultural understanding, interaction and cultural exchange has led to intolerance towards any form of cultural difference, which in turn has made consensus and compromises amongst the different factions of society appear to be an almost impossible task.

The increasing restriction in the society existent in the state has made it impossible to address multiple cultures and acknowledge and accept these differences. Contestations for identity are ironically not only a commonplace occurrence but are also an accepted norm today. At the centre of these experiences lies the idea of 'indigeneity' through which the ethnic community has structured an image of the self that more often than not lies in a state of contradiction from the 'settler communities', who are then later labelled as the 'outsider'. This phenomenon of the ethnic community branding the 'settler groups' as the 'outsiders' has resulted in ugly contestations that breed mistrust and anxiety among both the contesting factions and results in even cultural spaces coming under the line of fire as each group tries to dominate and eliminate the presence of the other.

The so-called 'outsiders' or 'settlers' migrated in two distinct waves to the state of Meghalaya – one group migrated before 1947, and the other group came in search of refuge in the midst of a violent partition. The dominant discourse of representation prevalent went on to place them at the lowest scales of social and political hierarchy and perpetuated social images that went on to identify and brand them as 'outsiders'. It is then but natural that they went on to be excluded from being active actors in the creation of the new history of the newly formed state of Meghalaya.

Increasingly the 'outsiders' went on to experience an alienation from the larger society, even though many members of the community having been born and brought up in the Khasi society, and often not even able to read and write in their mother-tongue, and more comfortable conversing in the local language were secluded from the larger canvas of the society. These 'outsiders' experience a feeling of alienation with people of their own community residing in other parts of the country, as their subjective experiences in no way intersect or bear any similarities with those of the larger community. Experiencing a state of double alienation, the 'outsider' cannot help but wonder if their identity is an ambiguous one, precariously balanced on the scales of the 'insider-outsider' politics.

The condition of the 'insider', the so-called 'true Khasi' is not any better. One cannot be sure if the non-Christian Khasi who claims to be true to his roots, his culture and tradition is the actual Khasi, or if the Christian Khasi who having embraced the tenets of Christianity and western education and moving ahead in the realms of social, economic and political sphere is the true native of the hills, an ethnic Khasi. This dilemma that the Khasi society today finds itself in can perhaps be best understood through the figure of Dimple, the proprietor of a Muslim food shop in Shillong, who speaks both English and Khasi fluently, and to any queries about her identity calmly replies, "We're Khasi Muslims and people often don't know what language to speak with us, least of all what to make of us." Belonging to a Muslim family who migrated from Sylhet to Shillong during the British times, and having been born, raised and lived in the city all her life, Dimple considers herself nothing but a Khasi, even though she is a burqa-clad woman whose ancestry can be traced to present Bangladesh and erstwhile undivided India.[2]

It was just after six years of the formation of the state of Meghalaya that Shillong encountered violent riots between the settler and the dominant ethnic groups. The Nepalis, Bengalis and Assamese became the victims of racial attacks and unmitigated violence as they came to be viewed as a threat to the local people, their resources and opportunities. It became important in the mind of the ethnic community, insecure in their positions viewed the 'settlers' or 'migrants' as a great threat to become the central dominating force in the social, political and economic field.

It is as a consequence that today a significant section of the Bengali community has shifted base to the so-called safe places in successive waves that reduced their visible presence in the new state. The irony is that these supposedly safe places became sites of communal riots and were places where they were denied residency as the migrants, though members of the same community, were not indigenous residents. Many migrants have thus gone on to experience riots in places like Silchar in the Cachar district of Assam, and in other instances been denied access to privileges including jobs in places like West Bengal on the grounds that they were non-indigenous Bengalis.

Conclusion

Today the presence of a few socio-cultural associations like the Bangya Sahitya Parishad and a poorly developed civil society are the only expressions of the collective Bengali consciousness in the state. Most youngsters of the community growing up in Shillong are unaware of their 'Bengaliness' and do not often know how to read or write the script and therefore for all practical purposes are far removed from the cultural connectedness of the larger community that they on migrating to the so-called safe places wish to get assimilated into. With no firm ground to lay their roots in, home for these people continues to be not West Bengal or Bangladesh, but Shillong. They are the uprooted people, the people of nowhere, existing as islands of their own while negotiating their way in a world where they are forever the 'settlers' or the 'others'. They are a people who neither are a part of the collective consciousness of the larger Bengali community while at the same time being denied the space to exist on an equal ranking socially and politically with the ethnic dominant groups of the places they have migrated to. The settlers thus continue to be just that 'settlers' forever experiencing an existential dilemma negotiating their identity to suit the landscape of the space they now occupy.

Notes

1. It was mentioned by Anjum Hasan in her interview with Sangeeta Barooah Pisharothy of *The Hindu* on January 6, 2008. For more please see, http://www.hindu.com/lr/2008/01/06/stories/2008010650240500.html
2. As mentioned by Janice Pariat in *A Gap in the Clouds: Of Khasi Muslims In Meghalaya*, The North East Blog. May 21, 2012.

References

Dev, Rajesh. 2006. 'Narratives Claims and Identity Impasse: The Experiences of the Nowhere People', in S. Bhattacharjee and R. Dev (eds), *Ethno-narratives: Identity and Experience in North-East India*. New Delhi: Anshah Publishing House, 79-91.

Ghai, Yash. 2000. 'A Framework for Analysis', in Yash Ghai (ed.), *Autonomy and Ethnicity: Negotiating Competing Claims in Multi-ethnic States*. Cambridge University Press.

Guha, A. 1977. Planter-Raj to Swaraj: Freedom Struggle and Electoral Politics in Assam, 1826-1947. New Delhi: Indian Council of Historical Research.

Hasan, Anjum. 2007. *Lunatic in My Head*. New Delhi: Zubaan.

Ludden, D. 2003. 'Political Maps and Cultural Territories', *Himal*, July 16, 50-53.

Pariat, Janice. 2012. *Boats on Land*. New Delhi: Random House

Williams, Robins. 1964. *Strangers Next Door: Ethnic Relations in American Communities*. New Jersey: Prentice Hall Inc.

4

Between the Hills and the Valleys

A Search for 'Nepali'[1] identity in Manipur

Dolly Limbu

The complex contours of Nepali identity in Manipur is mapped and examined here. In the light of the inner line permit movement, it becomes critical to explore the Manipuri 'Nepali' identity. The dearth of academic work on the community posits a serious impediment in understanding the community which has largely been excluded from the local political discourses. A trajectory on ethnic identity in the state is laid threadbare in order to understand the intersection between ethnic identity and political empowerment. The conscious erasure of ethnic identity leads to the production of homogenised 'Nepali' identity. In the context of the northeastern states of India including Manipur, ethnic identity has evolved as the cornerstone for political representation and social mobilisation. At such backdrop, the homogenised 'Nepali' identity becomes a convenient tool of producing generalised and close-ended narratives on the 'Nepalis' of Manipur. Attempt is made to historically and socially locate the lacuna in addressing to 'Nepali' identity in Manipur. The matrix of Nepali/ Nepalese binary is another hindrance in posturing the 'Nepali' identity in Manipur. Their sense of 'being' and 'becoming' in Manipur is overlapped and contested by the sense of 'belonging'. This issue clubbed with the approval of the Manipur People Bill, 2018 further problematises and complicates the rubric of Nepali identity in the context of Manipur,

Statement of the Problem

The term identity has been wide-ranging in its definitions and many times has proven to be slippery when broken down into categorisation. The scope of identity studies is ever evolving and the meaning of identity cannot be condensed into a singular definition. According to Steph Lawler, 'identity' answers the age-old question of "I am who I am" (2014). Lawler suggests that an individual seeks to understand itself and the social world in relation to shared history and cultural manifestations. However, one needs to understand that the nature and significance of identity vary in terms of time and space. The slipperiness of defining identity in the post-modern era comes from the discursive polemics that embodies the extensive corpus of identity studies. The reading of identity and its politics are primarily demonstrated through the categories of race, gender, ethnicity, sexuality, culture and geographical setting. Therefore, the nature of identity is multi-faceted in its rendering and mutually intersects with several categories at a time.

By undertaking the complex rubric of identity, the paper seeks to address the nature of 'Nepali' identity in Manipur. The colonial discourse on the 'Nepali' identity has largely been myopic. The community has been synonymous with military race as the large populations of soldiers from the community were recruited in the erstwhile British-India military forces. The paper attempts to map the evolution of the complex contours of 'Nepali' identity and its intricacies. An attempt will be made to stage a critical intervention in locating the fissures in identity politics in the state. The study becomes challenging as the earliest known settlement of Nepalis in Manipur has been traced back to the early nineteenth century, going back to 1824.

The 'Nepali' of Manipur

Manipur shares its border with Myanmar. Often considered to be an enigma, it has its fair share of colonial history. Having thrived under the rule of monarchy for several centuries, it was annexed by the British in 1891. The British rule monetised the feudal economy for the first time but however, the wave of the development was just restricted to the reformation of taxation policies. With the passage of time, it emerged as the 'backwaters of the British Raj' (Barucha, 1992). After India became independent, Manipur became a princely state. However, two years later, its legislative assembly was dissolved. It was ceded to India and was considered a Part C state which was directly controlled by the central government (Singh 2013). The lack of infrastructure and development resulted in a series of movements connected to secessionism and ethnic identity in the late 1960's. Finally, Manipur became a state in 1972. Being subjected to legislation like the Armed Forces (Special Powers) Act, 1958 and the Foreigners (Protected Areas) Order of 1958, it is considered to be one of the restrictive places in the country.

Manipur has diverse ethnic groups; the valley is mainly populated by the Meiteis and Meitei Muslims, and the hills by the Kukis and the Nagas. According to the 2011 census, the population stands at 2,721,756, out of which Nepalis are believed to be 60,000 strong. Nepalis vis-a-vis Gurkha Regiments entered Manipur as the protector of the Manipuri frontiers in the late nineteenth century. According to Srikant Dutt, the royal court in Manipur gained financially by granting land for Nepali settlement (Dutt 1981). With the passage of time, they adapted with the customs and tradition of the land. It is also suggested that Nepali settlements were possible only through migration, largely driven by the posting of Gorkha troops across the state. Korengei, Chingmeirong, Pangei, Mantripukhri, and several villages in Senapati district, which were the earliest recorded places of their settlement. Some of them introduced grazing and cattle rearing on the hills (Shiwakoti 2009).

In fact, one of the first printed books in the history of Manipuri literature, *Manipurko Sawai* (1894) was written by a Nepali poet Tulachand Ale. The anthology of poems discusses and explores the landscapes and beauty of Maram, a village located in the hill district of Senapati. The Nepalis settled on the hills of Manipur are known to be pastoralist and agriculturist. Today, the population dominates the production of both Kharif and Rabi crops in Senapati district. According to Vijaylakshmi Brara (2016), the presence of Nepalis in government services in Manipur is abysmal. Their absence had been narrowed down to low literacy rate and challenging economic conditions. She suggests, "As a matter of fact, keeping this in mind, the Manipur State Assembly passed resolutions twice in 1954 and 1980, to put Gorkhas in the category of backward and minority community" (Brara, 2016). When the final list of Other Backward Caste list[2] came out, the Nepalis felt betrayed, as only five castes Badi, Damai, Gainay, Kami, and Sarki, who have been living in Manipur as members of the domiciled community since July 1947, and their descendants, were recommended, which constitutes less than five per cent of the Nepali population. Their exclusion from such platforms needs to be addressed and bears larger social, political and economic implications to the community that has settled in the state for more than a century.

The 'Nepali' academia such as Lopita Nath (2003, 2006), J.R. Subba

(2008), Mahendra P. Lama (1994), Pannalal Dhar (1998), Andrew Simpson (2007), Sharma (2012), have extensively deliberated on the question of 'Nepali' settlement in Arunachal Pradesh, Assam, West Bengal, Meghalaya, Mizoram and Sikkim. Discourses on erstwhile Gorkha National Liberation Front (GNLF) movement and the demand for the Gorkhaland in Darjeeling have been voiced in the scholarly writings of T.B. Subba (1992, 2003, 2016), A.C. Sinha (1982, 2003, 2016) and Sajal Nag (1990, 2002), Bagchi (2012) to name a few.

The marginal representation of the 'Nepalis' belonging to Manipur, in academia is an offshoot of the scattered pattern of 'Nepali' settlement in the state coupled with the gradual inflow of Nepalese from Nepal and other parts of India. The writings on 'Nepali' diaspora by K.L. Pradhan (2009), Rajendra P. Dhakal (2009, 2015), Miriam Wenner (2015) delves with the concepts of Nepali nationalism, which has been appropriated as a binding force of Nepali subjectivity. Writings by Col. Shakespeare (1929), L. Caplan (1995), Imdad Hussain (1998), Colonel H.E. Weekes (2011), have provided a considerable groundwork in the colonial discourse on the Gorkha Regiment as the 'martial race'. However, the dearth of debates on the ethnicity of the 'Nepalis' in the academia is something that needs serious reflection.

Historically, the colonial construction of the Gorkhas as a martial race provides a strategic entry point for understanding the politics of their migration. The paper will attempt to re-think the historical and cultural appropriation of the 'Nepali' population and such readings will lay bare the discursive trope of identity, its slippage, fissures and fruition. The colonial image of 'Nepalis' had been reduced either to the figure of peasant or grazer which can be attributed to their traditional occupation (in Nepal) or that of a soldier. It was the British who allowed only the 'Nepalis' to settle in Manipur and to undertake *Khas* land.[3] The other settlers and migrant population from India in Manipur were exempted from such provision (Dutt 1981). However, it is an image of 'Gorkhas' as the martial race that has gained more currency and captured the imaginaries of the 'Nepalis/Nepalese' across the world.

The *Kukhri*[4] which became a symbol of 'Nepali' soldier's courage, nonetheless rooted in the history of violence has in the post-colonial times translated its presence in a form of *Kukhri* dance, performed by the 'Nepali' youth in special occasions of *Tihar*[5] and *Dashain*[6], to name a few. Such practices represent to some degree the post-colonial melancholia of the imagined community, rationalising its state of homelessness. Interestingly, the settlement of 'Nepalis' during the colonial period to the northeast region is attributed to the recruitment of the 'Nepali' soldiers in the British-Indian military and armed forces which can be traced back to 1816.

The Anglo-Gorkha War (1814-16) was a watershed event in the history of Nepal. The British Raj found a powerful and strong ally in the same soldiers whom they once had fought against. The Anglo-Burmese War (1824-26), furthered the process of recruitment of the Nepali soldiers. Imdad Hussain (2003) opines that the food habits of the Nepalese were one of the major reasons for their recruitment. The 'Nepalese' were primarily rice-eaters, which was much cheaper in comparison to wheat. However, this is not a conclusive reason for their recruitment. Colonel Pollock and W. S. Thom, suggest that the Gorkhas were primarily recruited by the British government to defend the frontiers. Since the frontiers such as the then Northeast and Upper Burma were inhospitable due to high elevations and difficult terrains, it was reported to be unfavourable and unfit for native sepoys. Gorkhas whose homes in Nepal were at elevation for more than 10,000 feet were fit to be recruited for the region (Pollock and Thom, 1900).

So unprecedented was the recruitment, that according to the census of 1941, Nepal provided 45 per cent of the foreign immigrants to India. There have been several historical records tracing their earliest settlement in Manipur. The Assam District Gazetteer (1909) confers that the Manipuri Royal Court granted land for Nepali settlement (Brara, 2016). In 1913, the fourth Assam Rifles shifted from Dibrugarh to Imphal (Bareh, 2007). A whopping 80 per cent of the regiment comprised persons of the Nepali descent. In fact, the 4th or the Darrang Battalion (which comprised 50 per cent of Nepali soldiers) transferred to Manipur during the Kuki Uprising (1917-18) and was permanently stationed thereafter (Hussain, 2003).

In the context of the Northeast, Nepali settlement was accelerated by the establishments of Gorkha training sites and rehabilitation centres. According to A.C. Sinha, the Gorkha training centres were located in and around district towns and strategic locations on the hills. After the completion of their service, as many as three thousand ex-soldiers were rehabilitated by the British from almost forty sites for their re-settlement. It is worth noting, that thirteen of such sites were situated in Assam, eight in Manipur, seven in both Mizoram and Nagaland, three in Arunachal Pradesh and one each at Meghalaya and Tripura (Sinha, 2007). Some of these sites include Sadiya in Assam, Mantripukhri in Manipur, Aizwal in Mizoram and Mokokchung in Nagaland.

Ethnicity and Identity

According to Thomas Hylland Eriksen, ethnicity is "made relevant through social encounters and situations" (Erikson, 2010). He suggests that the presence of ethnicity signifies positive group identification. Therefore, its relevance in producing and creating meanings related to collective identity should never be undermined. Ethnic identity quantifies an individual into a particular group thus arriving at one's distinctiveness. Ethnicity forges social relationships between people and extends itself towards the realm of social identity since it becomes a signifier of kinship either literal or abstract. Thus, he suggests that ethnicity has political, social organisational and symbolic significance (Erikson, 2010). Erikson introspects on how ethnicity, when combined with the idea of nationalism, changes it meaning and is reified since the focus shifts from nationhood to ethnic distinctiveness thus reducing it to the level of restricted cultural products.

Nepali identity, unlike the other ethnic groups in the state, has been cast as problematic and complex. This convolution in perceiving Nepali identity can be to the colonial legacy of equating the Nepali settlers with foreigners which consequently has resulted in the rampant generalisations between the Indian 'Nepalis' and the 'Nepalese' nationals. This predicament in the identity crisis can be attributed to the Treaty of Peace and Friendship between India and Nepal in 1950 which allows the Nepalese to move freely and acquire property in India but the same rule does not apply to the 'Nepali' of Indian origin in Nepal.

Whilst, the ethnic identities of the hill communities (the Nagas and the Kukis) and that of the dominant communities in the valley (the Meiteis and the Meitei Pangals[7]) are clearly marked, understood and unchallenged. The Nepali community, perhaps, lacks the foundation and agency in comparison to the aforementioned communities. Therefore, it becomes relevant to understand and study the significance of ethnicity in forming and asserting distinctive group identities. The lack of such debates consolidates the 'Nepali' ethnicity to be homogenous, baring the states of Sikkim and West Bengal, where the Nepali ethnicity is well marked and given due recognition. The omission of such identification of Nepali ethnicity in other states has furthered the mould of Nepali/Nepalese binary. Ch. Sekholal Kom (Kom, 2010), suggests that the mobilisation of communities on basis of ethnicities has trickled into the political arena of the northeastern part of the country and Manipur is no exception to this reality.

Militancy is seen as the main byproduct of ethnic differences and has evolved as a repressive bargaining power with the passage of time. Therefore, one must understand the significance of ethnicity in the state and downplaying the Nepali ethnicity card has had serious repercussion to the community. The lack of 'the ethnicity question' within the rubric of Nepali identity at the larger sense is to be blamed for the dichotomy the community has to face. According to Prasenjit Biswas and Chandan Suklabaidya, the usage of terms such as 'homeland', 'indigeneity' and 'tribal identity' etc., produce a sense of well-defined 'self' opposed to 'others' (Biswas and Chandan, 2007). The lack of the recognition of ethnic identity amongst the 'Nepalis' of Manipur can be seen as a systematic tool of othering them and creating narratives for them where they have no agency to assert themselves.

Willem van Schendel in his book, *The Bengal Borderland: Beyond State and Nation in South Asia*, suggests that borderlands are historical reality and to a larger degree in South Asian countries it has cemented the internalisation of national identities. In this context, Schendel's work helps in theorising the construct of 'Nepali' identity in Manipur which is understood of far from being uniform but varies in terms of geographical position and social condition. The divide between the hill and the valley, 'Nepali' population will be attested with the help of Schendel's concept of 'Borderlands' (Schendel, 2005). For Schendel, borders not only determine physical stratifications, but its imposition creates identities that go beyond the idea of 'nation-state'. Therefore, the 'borderlands' theory suggests that boundaries create 'social relationships' and extensively thread on the domain of cultural transactions and the social landscape they generate. The internalisation of 'territorial' space eclipses even the 'iron grip of nation-state', which can shed some light in understanding how the distinctive identities within the 'Nepali' population are produced in Manipur. In this context, the anthropological study of the Nepalis in a village of Kanglatombi in Manipur by Hari Krishna Shiwakoti is relevant. He proposes that the population internalises the eating habits, language and other customs of the Meiteis. Such appropriation of customs is also reflected in inter-community marriages and changing nature of kinship. This study sheds light on how the Nepali tradition accommodates new values while keeping its practices culturally divergent. However, Nepalis demand for the native status in the state has been rejected and many still face prejudices and are labeled as foreigners. The binary of 'Nepali/Nepalese' identity has caused a deep-seated anxiety amongst the Nepali youth whose regional identity is reduced to sweeping generalisations. One needs to understand that the concept of Nepali nationalism for the Nepalis of Manipur is largely tokenistic and exists in form of nostalgia, more as historical and cultural relics.

Taking a cue from Benedict Anderson's *Imagined Communities: Reflections on the Origin and Spread of Nationalism*, one can concede that defining nationalism is challenging. His writing implies that the concept of nationalism has evolved as an ideology over time. The nations across the world are rattled with the issue of sub-nationality within its borders. His writing, therefore, becomes fundamental in understanding the inter-ethnic politics in Manipur. Ethnicity becomes a cornerstone of sub-nationality (community) which bears more relevance than nationality (state/nation). Social and political movement and reformation are mobilised on the basis of ethnic and regional identities. The failure to recognise such identity will result in de-legitimisation of a community. Anderson sees nationalism as a historical process and deems it as cultural artefact of a particular kind. He defines a nation as such, "an imagined political community — and imagined as both inherently limited and sovereign" (Anderson, 2006). Therefore, the lack of agency to address the lacuna in Nepali identity in Manipur has resulted in prejudices and misinformed debates. This duality of the 'Nepali/Nepalese' identity matrix complicates and creates 'imagined communities' in search of identity and homeland, real or imagined. The identity crisis and the sense of homelessness faced by them need larger introspection.

The GNLF[8] attempted to marginally contest the identity crisis by replacing the word 'Nepali' with that of 'Gorkha'. Our research also attempts to contest the usage of the blanket term 'Gorkha' or 'Nepali' for the community which is 'historically, racially, culturally and religiously divergent' (Subba, 2003). Reginald Hodder (1914), who documented the history of Indian native regiments in British India, stated that the word 'Gurkha' was a geographical rather than ethnic category. The term 'Gurkha' suggested the inhabitants of the locality known as 'Gurkha' in Nepal, named after a famous *yogi*, Gurkhanath. In Nepal, the 'Nepalese' identify themselves on the basis of their ethnic groups but in India, the 'Nepalis' are identified by the blanket term, 'Nepali' or 'Gorkhas'. According to A.C. Sinha, Nepali/ese is divided into three broad groups namely the *Thakuris*, the *Newars* and the *Kiratis*. The *Thakuris* are Hindus that settled in Nepal from India and have a fourfold caste system. The practice of purity and pollution is prevalent among them. The *Newar* practice either Hinduism or Buddhism and have their system of language, art and architecture. They are also divided into several castes. The *Kiratis* are considered as the earliest settlers of Nepal. They are endogamous tribes who practise animism or Buddhism. Ethnologically, they are closer and similar to the tribes of Northeast India (Sinha, 2003).

Thus, when GNLF or other institutions like the Gorkha Students Union across India uses the term to assert the political identity of its community, it unintentionally legitimises the 'Nepalis' as a homogenous community. Our research will also challenge such attempt for collective identity that does not address the slippery nature of identity but re-enforces stereotypes. In fact, understanding the dynamics of the ethnic identity of the 'Nepalis' in Manipur will be one of the main purposes of this research. Lopita Nath (2005) concurs that the trap of 'double homeland'[9] makes the Nepali a soft target during ethnic conflict and violence. She refers to the violence that Nepali community was subjected to at the wake of, 'son of the soil' movement in Assam, popularly known as the Anti-Foreigner Movement (1979-85). Since the categorisation of a foreigner was sketchy, several tribes and Nepali community were affected by it leading to deportation and destruction of properties. The open borders have proven to be an impediment to Indian 'Nepalis' and the narratives of the internally displaced 'Nepalis' due to such conflicts finds negligible representations.

Political Representation in Manipur

In the assessment of Nepali representation in Manipuri politics, their presence has been abysmal. The community at the state level had only one MLA, Kishore Thapa from Kangpokpi constituency till date, who served three consecutive terms at 1974, 1980 and 1984. In fact, his victory in the second term coincided with the 'Anti-Foreigner Movement' in Manipur. Thapa's victory had added to the growing resentment amongst the Kuki and the Meitei student bodies against the 'outsiders' as they been analysing and motivated by the similar movements in Assam.[10] In 1980, about 2000 Nepalis fled Manipur and around 300 houses were burnt down, as the aftermath of the violence unleashed in the name of 'Anti-Foreigner

Movement'. It is observed that the mobilisation of people on ethnic lines and resurgence of indigenous politics has marred the political aspirations of the Nepalis at the state level politics. As a result, the Nepali candidates were threatened, intimidated and forced to cancel their nominations by the 'indigenous' population. Interestingly, in 2017, an independent Nepali candidate, Khadga Bahadur Tamang, had to abandon his ticket from the Congress party due to the growing controversy against his candidature.[11] At the backdrop of the inner line permit movement, his Nepali identity has become the litmus test for the growing fear of the 'outsider/foreigner'. Thus, the citizenship of the Nepali candidate is a regular subject to suspect during elections. The matrix of 'Nepali/Nepalese' has been continuously used to delegitimise their rights on regular basis. However, the Nepali population acts as buffer in some constituencies whereby their votes determine the fate of the candidates at Serou, Sekmei and Kangpokpi (Idetombi, 2002). At the village level, the Gram Panchayat acts as the purveyor for addressing the social issues of the community. The issues related to the welfare of the community is been taken up by such body. Their student body, The All Manipur Nepali/Gorkha Students' Union, established at 1967 had actively worked on the inclusion of Nepali language in the Eighth Schedule and demanded the inclusion of Nepali as a discipline at government schools and colleges. Colleges like G.P. Womens College and D.M. College of Arts were the first to introduce it. The body has also consistently raised the issue of the Nepali/Nepalese identity matrix and works positively towards protecting the rights of their community.

Inner Line Permit Movement

Inner line permit is an official travel document that is required to enter protected areas. It is derived from the Bengal Eastern Frontier Regulation, 1873. Till date, it has been issued in Arunachal Pradesh, Mizoram and Nagaland (excluding Dimapur). At the outset of the movements triggered by the demand for the enactment of inner line permit in Manipur, it becomes significant to address the making and un-making of regional identities. In 2015, the state legislative assembly passed three Bills in order to protect the indigenous people of the state. They were: (a) The Protection of Manipur People Bill, 2015, (b) The Manipur Land Revenue and Land Reforms (Seventh Amendment) Bill, 2015, and (c) The Manipur Shops and Establishments (Second Amendment) Bill, 2015. One of the Bills namely, The Protection of Manipur People Bill, 2015 set the settlement till the year 1951 as a cut-off date to recognise the 'Nepalis', and many other communities as the legitimate settlers of the state. The legislation would be extended to the whole state. It defined Manipuri people as 'persons of Manipur' whose names are in the National Register of Citizen of 1951, Census Report of 1951 and Village Directory of 1951, and their descendants.[12]

In regard to the Bills, the president of Gorkha Youth and Students' Association (GYASA), Dinesh Sharma[13] reflected on the grave implications of identifying the 'Nepali' population in Manipur as per the 1951 census. The historic ties between the 'Nepalis' and the soil of Manipur cannot be reduced to the designated timeframe. In fact, the census of 1951 left out sizeable 'Nepali' population residing in far-flung areas and as such it should not be considered as a credible historical document for such assessment. Similar concerns were voiced by the Manipur Gorkha Welfare Union, Manipur in a feature article, titled, 'The truth about Gorkhas in Manipur'. The article attempts to dispel the accusations against the population of being the encroacher of land. By suggesting that the 'Nepali' settlement in some areas of Kangpokpi predates tribal settlement, the association urges the need to analyse the population that has been left out from the regional dialogue. The article also tries to combat with that the malicious information spread in local dailies suggesting the population of 'Nepalis' in Manipur have crossed three lakhs in the year 2001. Such ill-informed reporting poses a serious threat to the integrity of the Nepali community. The fact that the population of 'Nepalis' over the span of one hundred and fifty years has gradually increased to 50,000 in 2001 suggests that "who are presently living in the state are the descendants of those forefathers who were bonafide citizens of Manipur".[14] The President of India in 2016 did not give his assent to one of the Bills and the other two were rejected.[15]

Manipur People Bill, 2018

In May 2018, the Manipur government formed a state-level committee, to set the 'Protection of Manipuri People' Bill in motion. The drafting committee consisted of legislators from both ruling and opposition bench. Since the committee comprised of the Naga, Kuki, Meitei and Meitei Pangals[16] representatives, it was felt that only the vested interest of major stakeholders was represented. The nature and the outcome of the Bill have been problematic as alleged by the linguistic and ethnic minorities of the state. The Manipur People Bill, 2018 was passed, without any resistance in the state legislative assembly. The article 'Inner Line Permit: A Genuine Idea Lost in Translation',[17] asserts that the contentious aspect of the Bill has been the definition of 'Manipur people' and 'Non-Manipur people'. The Bill defines 'Manipur people' as "all the native people of Manipur who are citizens of India and includes all communities viz. Meitei/Meetei, Meitei Pangal, Scheduled Tribes as listed under the Constitution (Scheduled Tribes) Order, 1950 and Scheduled Castes and Scheduled Tribes Orders (Amendment) Act" and "any person/persons who are citizens of India and have been permanently residing and settled in the state before 1951, and their descendants who are living in Manipur as on the date of commencement of this Act". The 'Non-Manipur' is defined as those people who have settled in Manipur after 1951. This schism in the construct of Manipuri citizenship/identity goes beyond political appeasement and becomes a matter of fact way of denying the linguistic minority from asserting their agency. In fact, the state lays out a well-defined idea of *self* in contrast to that of the *other*, this conscious coupling of *self/Other* is based on the idea of ethnic identity and indigeneity, whereby the construct of *Other* becomes synonymous with that of an outsider/foreigner. The Bill has used indigeneity to define and legitimise the native on status for certain population whereas in the context of certain linguistic minorities the base year 1951 has been used as a touchstone method to guarantee their citizenship. Such clause does not recognise the historical settlement and migration of some communities like that of Nepali, Punjabis, Biharis and few others that go beyond a century. In fact, some communities and their descendants have lost all ties with their erstwhile homeland and the inclusion of such clause in the Bill continues to associate them as the encroacher of the land. Such binaries create hostility and are reminiscent of the colonial device of divide and rule policy where one community is pitted against the other. It has been observed that a week within the passage of the Bill, several student bodies and civil organisations have started issuing 'Non Local identity cards' to the 'Non-Manipur' people across the valley and the hill districts. In Senapati district, individuals who have settled in the state prior to 1951 have also been asked to register oneself for 'Non-Local Registration Card'. The Nepali community today sees the Bill as an attempt to racially segregate them from 'Manipur people' and exclude them from the social, economic and political sphere of the state. The 'Non-Manipur' identity has been thrust upon them without consulting them or analysing their cultural and historical narratives.

According to Duncan McDuie-Ra, the inner line permit movement from its very inception has rested on the idea of indigenous identity (Duncan, 2016). It is understood that Manipur hosts a thriving population of different castes and tribes and during the inner line permit movement one of the organising committee like the United Committee Manipur (a valley based organisation) insisted on the assertion of indigenous identity, compartmentalising into categories such 'indigenous Meitei', 'indigenous tribes' etc. Such ambit of categorisation, he asserts, then, becomes a systematic device of exclusion and creates cultural historiography to push out the 'Non-Locals' from both urban and rural landscapes. The issue of identity cards to the 'Non-Locals'/'Non Manipur' people immediately after the passing of The Manipur People Bill, 2018 signifies the anxiety that the influx of migrant population has posited to the state. However, a mandatory registration of every 'Non-Manipur' people delegitimises their claim in the state. Interestingly, some ethnic tribes from other parts of the region who have migrated to Manipur till late 2000's but such population do not undergo the exclusionary policies enforced by both state and non-state actors. Thus, it begs a question whether the ethnic identity of the population dictates the indigenous politics of inclusion and exclusion. The legitimacy to inhabit space in the state, therefore, settles on the fractured and problematic definition of indigenous identity. Thus, the Manipur People Bill, 2018 rather than addressing the fissures of ethnic, regional, linguistic identities operating in the state, very conveniently restricts the rights of 40 per cent population of the state. The land and property rights of such population will be challenged with several checks and balances being imposed on them with times to come. When land, borders and boundaries determine one's sense of belonging, the ethnic and linguistic minorities of the state question their 'Manipuri identity' and if their history and narrative existed in a vacuum of time and space.

Conclusion

The identity of 'Nepalis' in Manipur has been highly contested and the community has been overlooked from regional discourses. Such lacuna can only be addressed when the community has political and economic agency. We have arrived at a critical juncture where we need to separate the overlapping 'Nepali/Nepalese' identity. The critical review of the Friendship Treaty of 1950 is one of the ways of safeguarding the rights of the 'Nepalis' of Manipur. Until and unless, the 'Nepalis' are identified by their ethnic identity they will be excluded from social, political and economic platforms. The convenient response of the larger civil society whenever movements like Anti-Foreigner Movement or Inner Line Permit have broken out, has been to generalise the entire population 'Nepalis' as 'foreigners'. Such repeated narrative is based on fear and the desire to protect the territorial integrity of the state. However, the anxiety of the local community is not unfounded as proven by the state of Tripura where the indigenous population is largely outnumbered by immigrant population. Therefore, the larger need of the hour is to tackle the issue with sensitivity and proper legislation, at the same time giving the communities that have settled in the state for centuries due recognition and charting out inclusive policies for them.

Notes

1. Taking a cue from T.B. Subba's essay, 'Nepalis in NE India: Political Aspirations & Ethnicity', from *The Nepalis in the Northeast India: A Community in search of Indian Identity*, (eds), A.C. Sinha and T.B. Subba. New Delhi: Indus Publishing Company. 2003, p. 56, the lexicon 'Nepali' will be used for identification of the Indian Nepali population as it represents 'culturo-linguistic denomination' while the word 'Nepalese' will be used to suggest 'the language and the people of Nepal'.
2. Manipur State Commission for Other Backward Classes, issued a notice on May 12, 2009, under Notification No.17/86/93-TD(Pt) dated 5/9/1994, http://obcwelfare.com/ Pdf/manipur.pdf.
3. *Khas* land is technically a government owned fallow land, therefore, no one can claim it as one's own property. The responsibility of allocating the land according to its uses lies within the jurisdiction of government.
4. Chris Bellemy in his book *The Gurkhas* attempts to break the stereotypes in the colonial historiography of the soldiers and broke the myth associated with the mighty weapon, *Kukhri*.
5. *Tihar* in its literal translation means festivity. It is equivalent to Indian festival of Diwali, festival of light.
6. *Dashain*, is one of the most popular and important festival and cultural event for the Nepalis. The ten day festival celebrates the victory of good over evil.
7. *See*, 'Farooque Ahmed, *Manipuri Muslims or Meitei Pangals*', 2002, http://www.milligazette.com/Archives/01072002/0107200259.htm (Accessed on October 10, 2017).
8. The GNLF is a political party based in Darjeeling (West Bengal), founded in 1980 demanding Gorkhaland statehood.
9. The culturo-linguistic identity becomes the only marker of an individual's identity thereby compromising one's political nationality.

10. 'Trouble in North-East escalates as Foreigner Agitation in Assam Spreads to Manipur', https://www.indiatoday.in/magazine/indiascope/story/19800531-trouble-in-north-east-india-escalates-as-foreigners-agitation-in-assam-spreads-to-manipur-821150-2014-01-28 (Accessed on January 10, 2018).
11. 'Nepali Hamlet in Kangpokpi Votes Against 'Foreigner' Tag', https://timesofindia.indiatimes.com/elections/assembly-elections/manipur/news/ nepali-hamlet-in-kangpokpi-votes-against-foreigner-tag/articleshow/57473677.cms (Accessed on February 12, 2018).
12. *See*, the Protection of Manipur People Bill, 2015.
13. Sharma, Dinesh, 'Manipuri Gorkhas: Why are we Outsiders,' http://www.ourstories.org.in/manipuri-gorkha-why-are-we-outsiders/ (Accessed on Jan. 14, 2018).
14. 'The Truth About Gorkhas in Manipur', http://www.thesangaiexpress.com/4447-the-truth-about-gorkhas-in-manipur/, (Accessed on Dec. 20, 2017).
15. 'Inner Line Permit will be introduced: Manipur CM', https://www.business-standard.com/article/news-ians/inner-line-permit-bill-will-be-introduced-manipur-cm-118050600507_1.html, (Accessed on May 14, 2018).
16. Initially the drafting Committee did not comprise of any Meitei Pangal representative however due to demands and rights asserted by the community, a Meitei Pangal MLA had been included later.
17. 'Inner Line Permit: A Genuine Idea Lost in Translation', http://thedarjeelingchronicle.com/inner-line-permit-a-genuine-idea-lost-in-translation/, (Accessed on Aug. 3, 2018).

References

Anderson, Benedict. 2006. *Imagined Communities: Reflections on the Origin and Spread of Nationalism*. London: Verso (First pub. 1983).

Bareh, H.M. 2007. *Encyclopedia of North-East India Volume III: Manipur*. New Delhi: Mittal Publications.

Bharucha, Rustom Bharucha. 1992. 'The Indigenous theatre of Kanhailal', in Clive Baker and Simon Trussler (eds.), *New Theatre Quarterly* 29: Vol. 8, Part 1, p 10, Cambridge University Press.

Biswas, Prasenjit and Chandan Suklabaidya. 2007. *Ethnic Life Worlds in North-East India: An Analysis*. New Delhi; Sage Publications.

Brara, Vijaylakshmi. 2016. 'Nepalis of Manipur from the perspective of 'cultural collective.' in A.C. Sinha and T.B. Subba (eds.), *Nepali Diaspora in a Globalised Era*. New Delhi: Routledge, 221-229.

Duncan, McDuie-Ra. 2016. *Borderland Cities in New India: Frontier to Gateway*. Amsterdam: Amsterdam University Press.

Dutt, Srikant. 1981. 'Migration and Development: The Nepalese in the Northeast', *Economic and Political Weekly*, 16(24), 1053-1055.

Erikson, Thomas Hylland. 2010. Ethnicity and Nationalism: Anthropological Perspectives, 3rd Edition, (First. Pub. 1994). New York: Pluto Press, 5.

Hussain, Imdad. 2003. 'Soldiers and Settlers: The recruitment of Gorkhas', in A.C. Sinha and T.B. Subba (eds), *The Nepalis in The Northeast India*. New Delhi: Indus Publishing Company, 67-105.

Idetombi, Kangabam Devi. 2002. *The Study of Socio-Cultural Life of Gorkhas*. Canchipur: Department of Anthropology, Manipur University, An Unpublished Ph.D thesis, 129.

Kom, Ch. Sekholal. 2010. 'Ethnic Mobilization and Militancy in Northeast India: A Case of Manipur,' *The Indian Journal of Political Science*, 71(3) (July - Sept), 869-879.

Lawler, Steph. 2014. *Identity: Sociological Perspectives* (Second Edition. Cambridge: Polity Press.

Nath, Lopita. 2005. 'Migrants in Flights: Conflict Induced Internal Displacement of Nepalis in Northeast India,' *Peace and Democracy in South Asia*, 1(1), January, 58.

Pollock, Colonel and W.S. Thom. 1900. *The Wild Sports in Burma and Assam*. London: Hurst and Blackett, 493-494.

Schendel, van Willem. 2005. *The Bengal Borderland: Beyond State & Nation in South Asia*. London: Anthem Press, 1-23.

Shiwakoti, Hari Krishna. 2009. *The Nepali Community in Kanglatombi: A Case-Study of Cultural Adaptation in Manipur.* Canchipur: Department of Anthropology, Manipur University, An Unpublished Ph.D thesis.

Singh, M. Amarjeet. 2013. 'Electoral Politics in Manipur: A Brief Survey', *Eastern Quarterly* 9 (I & II), Spring & Monsoon, 55.

Sinha. A.C. 2003. 'The Indians of Nepalese Origin and the Security of North East Region,' in A.C. Sinha and T.B. Subba (eds.), *The Nepalis in Northeast India: The Community in Search of Indian Identity.* New Delhi: Indus Publishing Company, 31-53.

Subba, T.B. 2003. 'Nepalis in NE India: Political Aspirations & Ethnicity', in A.C. Sinha and T.B. Subba (eds.), *The Nepalis in the Northeast India: A Community in Search of Indian Identity*. New Delhi: Indus Publishing Company, 56.

5

Relations Beyond Boundaries[1]

Rita Chakma

An ethnic group called 'Chakmas' lives in Tripura, Mizoram and Arunachal Pradesh and Bangladesh in large numbers, not to mention the others in different parts of the world in lesser numbers due to vocational diversity. Due to continuous movement from one place to another, one country to another, they had to accommodate and assimilate in different contexts, often finding their identity at stake. However, the bond shared by them living in different parts of the world has remained intact and revived in the recent past. Of late, religion (Buddhism) has played a catalyst to this revival of the slackened bond. At the same time, new religious and cultural ties are on the anvil due to various factors like the development of communication, technology, changes in socio-political situations etc. Here, author peeps into various aspects of this changing scenario among the Chakmas.

Today's cross-border activity in the socio-religious arena, barring the political and economic exchanges, cannot be termed as something new or alien development, but it is the continuation of what great historic personalities like Ashoka initiated; of course, the form and speed can be totally new phenomena. Author traces the transformative streams in socio-religious life of the Chakmas, especially in the light of migration and cross-border development in recent decades or so. The Chakmas ethnic group, who live in Tripura, Mizoram and Arunachal Pradesh and in Bangladesh, has been subjected to a long chequered historical treatment that was beyond their control; consequently, at present, they are having a multi-faceted identity. The focus here is on the Chakmas living in Tripura and Arunachal Pradesh with references to those living in other Indian states as well as in Bangladesh.

Tripura Context

The Chakmas are said to have migrated into Tripura even before the advent of the British when Tripura was under the royal rule. Those who migrated in those early days were naturally accommodated in the local tribal society or demographic texture. The post-partition history, however, had seen more of them in the status of refugees coming to take shelter in Tripura, barring a negligible number settling here and there in different times either through matrimonial alliances or in search of better livelihood prospects. In the post-partition era, being a border state Tripura has always faced the implications of cross-border human flow, openly or on the sly. In the twentieth century alone the state experienced two major waves of Chakma refugee influx in the wake of Kaptai hydel project followed by massive displacement of tribal people specially Chakmas in Bangladesh who ultimately passing through Tripura, got rehabilitated in Arunachal Pradesh in 1964 (Singh, 2010); and then secondly due to Islamic oppression and other reasons in the 1970s-1980s.

According to the 2001 Census, Chakma population in Tripura stood at 64, 293. Over the years residing with the other 18 tribes and non-tribes, they have had their share of socio-cultural transformation encompassing their religious life. Decades of co-existence since their arrival in the state in different phases have cast a visible impact on their lifestyle, beliefs and practices. Today as keen observation would detect traces of Hindu culture among the Chakmas of Tripura, so the shadow of alien culture could be recognised among those in Arunachal Pradesh and Mizoram. It is the dialectic between the structure and agency, a link between the individual and the social, as Pierre Bourdieu (2012) conceptualises it. The following passages would try to outline the process of cross-border exchange, migration and its impact and the consequent changes in the socio-religious life of the Chakmas.

Putting man-made boundaries has always failed to break inner bonds between human relations, the case of the Chakma migrants, in Tripura, Mizoram (which has a somewhat different story) or Arunachal Pradesh, has proved it again. For instance, when the last horde of Chakma refugees were repatriated in 1998 after spending over a decade in the refugee camps in Tripura, the residue of their long presence in an alien soil was left behind. Few of them had established matrimonial relations across the border thus enlivening the old relations. There are some cases of adoption also, of the children born in refugee camps; for those children, by now adult, nothing but India is home. This cross-border relation which was very sporadic in the pre-refugee influx period due to legal implications and inconvenient communication, got into further spurt due to a totally different reason later in the late 1990s — with the arrival of a religious leader Nandapal Mahasthavir who is said to be the prime disciple of Sadhanananda Mahasthavir (Bana Bhante), from Bangladesh an enlightened Buddhist monk, in 1999. In fact, since then began a new era in the religious scenario of the Chakmas of Tripura which extended farther in the following years.

In the following years, under their guidance, a number of *Bana Viharas*, a chain of Buddhist monasteries established by the disciples and followers of Bana Bhante, were established in Tripura and Arunachal Pradesh also. With this the psychological bond between the Chakmas in two countries found a new conduit to flow. Every year Buddhist monks from Bangladesh are coming to delight the religious practitioners in the Chakma society in Tripura and elsewhere. The seed of new religious fervour that was sown in Manikpur area of Longtharai Valley subdivision in Dhalai district of Tripura gradually started making an impact on the religious practices of the local Chakmas. Religious discourses of Nandapal Mahasthavir and his disciples have shown considerable latent function, in the guise of manifest activities. Many Chakma men have given up their vocations that went against Buddhist principles, in favour of what the Buddhist *bhikkhus* advised. Animal rearing, trade in animal and its flesh, sale and drinking of home-made liquor, all were made a past action in their life. Buddhist monks played their role as agents of change quite well. Perhaps that was one of the reasons that this new tradition found more followers among women than men. It was again a new phase of forming a new identity within the ambit of the existing structure. The process of creolisation that started with the first influx of refugees had now reached a new echelon through religious exchange and accommodation.

Now, how deep was its impact? It had a great impact on the socialisation of the children in families who had come under the spell of this new religious movement. When a few decades back it was unthinkable that young children would be doing all the religious stuff like prostrating/bowing before the Buddha as well as monks, is now a spontaneous behaviour for many children. That means the impact is being at a multi-generation level. Social customs are being twisted many times by the ardent followers of this new tradition resultantly changes coming in the marriage system, in daily life and other cultural arenas. As Max Weber (1968) saw a calling in the protestant life in Europe, so there came a motivation for a new type in the life of the Chakmas. Their social life and religious attributes began to be socially constructed anew as Peter Berger (1990) claims about the impact of social subjectivities getting objectivated through socialisation.

A different facet of this socialisation aspect sees many Chakmas still performing Hindu rites, revering Hindu gods and goddesses, still clinging to rites other than of Buddhist tradition. Durga Puja is considered a universal festival in Tripura which has so far had visibly cast a shadow on the exclusivity of the Chakmas' religious belief and attributes. Of course, this new Buddhist tradition has had negative repercussions too — a kind of resistance followed on the part of many local Buddhist monks. The divide arising out of social versus religious rituals is more visible in Pecharthal and Shantipur area of North Tripura district, field reports claim. In a recent flare-up, a guest-monk from Bangladesh could not be offered hospitality by the supporters as the opposition group (the followers of local monks who are more influential in Shantipur area) raised a vehement protest coupled with a warning of social boycott. These types of incidents are more often, than not, putting social solidarity at risk. On the other hand, when it comes to dealing with the non-Buddhist citizens of Tripura, the Chakmas are maintaining a harmonious relationship, dominantly with the Hindus.

Chakmas in Arunachal Pradesh

The story of the Chakmas in Arunachal Pradesh is somewhat different. They are the ones who had migrated in the wake of the construction of the Kaptai dam in Bangladesh in 1961. On being turned a blind eye to by the state government in Tripura for rehabilitation, the 35,000 somewhat refugees from Bangladesh were settled by the Indian leaders in the then North East Frontier Agency now Arunachal Pradesh in 1964 and afterwards. The woes of those olden days are still continuing in different forms at different times for those Chakmas. Their rights are yet to be established. Denial in granting first voting and then citizenship rights has become a bone of contention till date. The agony of a former Chakma leader Sneha Kumar Chakma who tried his level best to avert the award of Chittagong Hill Tracts to East Pakistan in the post-partition period and later on offered active solidarity with the Chakma refugees was expressed this way:

> The Bangladesh Government has turned us homeless. Even elsewhere our presence is undesired. In Arunachal Pradesh and other parts, people want us to quit. Even in Mizoram, a part of which is our homeland, the state government is bent upon harassing us (Chakma, D.K. n.d.).

Recently the Supreme Court of India in its judgement dated September 17, 2015 in Writ Petition (C) No.510/2007 directed the Government of India and the state of Arunachal Pradesh to implement its earlier judgement given in 1996 by processing the citizenship applications of the Chakmas and Hajongs who had migrated from erstwhile East Pakistan during 1964-1968 within three months (ACHR Press release, 2015). This verdict had generated repercussions among the local tribes and the state government with its throwing legal challenge and active protests coming up from different fronts. However, the Chakmas are hopeful of their future, more with this verdict. Support in favour of giving citizenship rights to them came from different quarters. In this context, Chunnu Prasad observes:

> Approximately 35,000 of these Chakmas were given valid migration certificates and settled in what was then the North East Frontier Agency, today the Arunachalese districts of Lohit, Changlang, and Papumpare. These migration certificates indicated legal entry into India and the willingness of the Government to accept the Chakmas as future citizens, much like migrants from Pakistan following partition. Nearly 1,000 members of the Hajong tribe, a Hindu group from the Mymensingh district of Bangladesh, were also settled in these areas and granted migration certificates. In the more than thirty years since their resettlement, the Chakmas and Hajongs have built villages, developed the land granted to them, and established strong ties to the region. Additionally, they have become integrated into the social fabric of the state of Arunachal Pradesh. They have voted in state elections and paid state taxes on their land. Many of these Chakmas and Hajongs, who now number about 65,000 persons, were born in India and know no other home. It is against this background that their claims for Indian citizenship are to be considered (Prasad, 2006).

It was the political status that has been contested by the local ethnic groups, mainly through the student's unions, on the justification that their identity as ethnic groups would ultimately be threatened in presence of such large number of 'outsiders'. Reportedly the discontent in an organised manner started brewing in 1975 when the Peoples' Party of Arunachal (PPA) raised the Chakma issue for the first time (Singh, 2010, 84), later on, to be reinforced by All Arunachal Pradesh Students' Union (AAPSU) in the early 1980s. Deepak Kumar Singh interestingly notes that although initially AAPSU wanted all foreigners living in the state to leave Arunachal Pradesh, later on, it started focusing its attention exclusively on the Chakmas as they alone were demanding citizenship (2010, 89). On the other hand, ACHR (2015) maintains that it was not the Chakmas and Hajong who posed threat to the indigenous people of Arunachal Pradesh, but the presence of other non-tribals like Adivasis, Assamese, Nepalese, Muslims, Marwaris, Biharis, etc. whose population had increased by 955 per cent in 50 years while the Chakma/Hajing had increased by 218 per cent in 47 years.

Identity at Stake

In the backdrop of the above it can be said that it is not just a political or economic crisis but also the clash of two cultures; the fear psychosis — whether or not one may obliterate the other in practice. It is the question of 'identity', 'self' versus 'other'. So, the struggle of the Chakmas for citizenship under the banner of the Committee for Citizenship Rights of the Chakmas of Arunachal Pradesh (CCRCAP) was not just a strive for political status but also to get rid of the 'refugee' tag, a derogatory identity for them. In fact, for the Chakmas, the question of identity, the notion of 'self' and the 'other' originated in Bangladesh itself soon after the partition. The term 'other', what Edward Said (1977) used to distinguish between the Orient and the Occident, a psychological attribute of the Western colonisers has always been ingrained in our society in different forms. Leader at the helm changed, during erstwhile East Pakistan and later in independent Bangladesh, and with the passing time the fate of these tribes got sliding down.

Earlier the British preferred to keep aloof from the internal affairs of the tribes of Chittagong Hill Tracts as the British were mainly concerned with revenue collection, the tribes including Chakmas living in Bangladesh enjoyed more or less a protected status (Lewin, 2007, 33). With the political upheaval following partition and the Indian independence, all went haywire for them. Economic and political reasons brought a large number of Bengali Muslims, who abhorred the lifestyle of the tribes (Singh 2010, 43), into the Chittagong Hill Tracts gradually making the indigenous hill tribes minority in their own land. Then in November 1972, came a blow to these people sharply jeopardising their identity even. The Bangladesh Parliament adopted a new constitution unilaterally imposing a common identity 'Bengali' on all the ethnic groups living in the country (Adnan, 2008). Their distinct identity, culture everything was threatened which ultimately led to the emergence of armed struggle for restoring their age-old rights. T.K. Oommen (2002, 100) also observes: "Indeed, the Constitution which Bangladesh adopted in 1972, soon after its emergence as an independent state, describes it as a secular and socialist. From 1975 onwards, however, the military regime of Bangladesh took definite steps towards Islamisation. This trend culminated in May 1988 when a bill was passed declaring Islam as the state religion of Bangladesh." These developments put the identity of tribes including Chakmas as a distinct ethnic group at stake.

So, now the question of 'other', after being forced out of Bangladesh, again surfaced for some 40,000 Chakmas in Arunachal Pradesh. Although the Furnbill's plural society recognises the existence of racially different collectivities, one native and the other alien (Oommen, 2002), it has its negative implications more than the positive. The suspicious trait flows from both sides — the native and the alien. In this case, also many stories corroborate such a situation in Arunachal Pradesh which can be termed as an indirect outcome of colonisation and de-colonisation. When the travails of migration were still afresh, the Chakma Buddhists in Arunachal Pradesh, while lacking political rights, were finding it difficult to negotiate with the social fabric made up of 26 major ethnic groups and over 110 sub-ethnic groups (Singh, 2010). The social gap between the host communities and the migrated Chakmas caused several misconceptions, as reported from the field. An example goes like this: MLA Nikh Kamin (who was not from Chakma-dominated area) once confessed that he was told by some indigenous people that the Chakmas embodied a demonic character with black-ugly attributes, ate all creatures including human beings and so on; this made him keep his family away from the Chakmas. Almost all the direct immigrants are still very nostalgic about Bangladesh which they fondly mention as *Desh* (native land) but are scared to go back. Some aged persons including a community leader from Shantipur area, Kripadhan Karbari, still recollected their painful journey to India, and experiences on the way to Arunachal Pradesh.

However, over the years sharing the same geographical landscape has forced the communities on two sides to forge a certain amount of accommodation through continuous interaction and exchange of ideas and resources, especially the market economy, language, some food habits etc. Matrimonial relations have also been reported, though not without opposition on both sides; educational and religious systems had to be shared, although on an unequal footing and not without discriminatory attitude. Admission of Chakma children into the school at Miao, a district town, was shut for a long time. One middle-aged woman from Diyun narrated the story of hospitality extended by the Tangsha tribe in her locality and how she had been a participant in a local cult. As per field reports (during my fieldwork in December, 2015), among the host tribes, Singpho and Khamtis, who by virtue of sharing the same religion Buddhism, have voluntarily attended the social ceremonies of the Chakmas more, than it is vice versa; the psychological drawback of being considered alien has always been at work for them as the host communities have hardly shown a warm reception into their social system. In such a situation, socio-religious ceremonies have played catalyst for maintaining in-group solidarity among the Chakmas. As Chunnu Prasad (2006) feels: "... in new environments migrations interact with local or host communities. Migration thus significantly affects individual and collective identities, and it creates new identities. Today the Chakmas of Arunachal have forged a new identity for themselves, identical to that of the Chakmas in Tripura, Mizoram or Bangladesh, yet dissimilar in many respects, in terms of socio-political as well as economic life-world."

New Trend in Cross-border Cultural Exchange

Religion has always been a strong factor in creating disintegration as well as solidarity as identified by Oommen (2002, 95-100) in the words: "And the insider-outsider polarisation of South Asian polities is said to be discerned mostly in terms of religion and even the state formation in post-colonial South Asia was based on religion." As mentioned earlier the coming of the Buddhist monks from Bangladesh under the aegis of *Bana Sangha* has also proved a trigger for this turn-around, not only in Tripura but also in Arunachal Pradesh. *Bana Viharas* are being set up there also and gathering experience of social distance within the society as has been the case in Tripura. With Nandapal Bhante gaining popularity among the Khamti and Singhpos also, the social gap between them and the Chakmas has been covered to some extent. Exchange of religious attributes is taking place. *Bana Bhikkhus* have been invited time and again by a Khamti leader Pintika Nam-sum to spend the rainy season in his forest retreat and this has always been respected by the other side.

Besides, the international and intra-national relations have been going through a different transformation of late. A new process of human exchange that is religious tourism is a popular concept nowadays with the increasing number of people taking up the voyage to various religious sites, thanks to the development of technology and communication network. Even at the beginning of the previous century, the scenario was totally different. This booming movement of people is not only satiating devotional thirst of pious folks but also boosting the economy to a great extent. Taking note of the gravity of the issue, the government organizes Mansarovar *yatra* for the Hindus every year. Defying all the hardships there is no dearth of takers for the trip; same with pilgrimage to other sites like Haridwar, Vaishnodevi, Varanasi and so on. Every year Mecca visit by the Indian Muslims is a big event to be tackled by the government, even special Air India resources are utilised for facilitating their pilgrimage to Mecca. For the Buddhists, although there is no such arrangement, however, at the organisational or institutional level similar processes are going on.

Two thousand and five hundred years ago, the Buddha himself did not prescribe any such component for his followers. Travelling on religious purpose was there but not for the lay devotees, it was the job of monks including Buddha himself. And in the absence of a present system of transportation, it is recorded that the Buddha accompanied by hundreds of his disciples used to apply his supernatural power (*hriddhi*) to travel hundreds of miles in a blink of an eye to preach his tenet. Now, it is the religious tourism that prompts the believers to take up long trips to sites of importance as per the Buddhist belief system. Bodhgaya, among all the Buddhist holy sites, tops the list for the Buddhists including Chakmas while selecting a pilgrimage site. After this come in the list are — Lumbini in Nepal, Saranath, Kushinagar and Shravasti in Uttar Pradesh, Nalanda and Rajgir in Bihar and so on. Not only Indians but Buddhists from Thailand, Sri Lanka, Bangladesh, Myanmar, Vietnam, Japan, Cambodia, etc. also line up to get a view of Bodhi tree in Bodhgaya or pay respect to the mentioned sites.

Following this type of reverence has developed a new international relationship between India and countries having sizeable Buddhist population. All these countries have ventured to establish their own set-up in Bodhgaya or other places building monasteries. Through these monasteries and the pilgrimage taken up by the people of these countries, the volume of commercial transactions has gone up manifold. Special package tours are also in operation in many places. Sometimes these countries have their own packages, sometimes they avail of local packages. The Chakmas of Tripura organised a huge package tour to Bodhgaya after the arrival of Nandapal Bhante in January 2002. That was the time the Chakmas of entire Tripura came to interact and work together for a purpose as it involved months of preparation and propaganda. The integrity, religious solidarity was displayed through this one trip for a holy cause. Many people who did not dare to initiate a trip to Bodhgaya on their own had a chance to participate when it was organised collectively. The trip to Bodhgaya, in the long run, laid the foundation of growing activities of the Chakma Buddhists, which ultimately led to the establishment of Bodhgaya Bana Vihar under the leadership of Nandapal Bhante.

The rising cross-border religious and social exchanges in relation to the Chakma society, in general, can be attributed to the advancement made in the field of technology and communication also. The advent of the telephone, mobile phones, internet, speedy transport systems and improved road connectivity have facilitated the coming of religious messengers into this country in recent years. Now foreigners encompassing monks and lay devotees are targeting not only Bodhgaya and other places of pilgrimage but also Tripura and Arunachal Pradesh and Mizoram. Buddhist monks from Thailand have paid several visits to Tripura and other northeastern states. They are always curious to know about the culture, food habits, religious habits and so on, of the people of this region.

In the recent past, Tripura, Assam and Arunachal Pradesh saw the arrival of a team of Buddhist monks from Sri Lanka. In 2015, a group of four monks from Sri Lanka led by Visuddhananda Sthavir spent several days in different places of Tripura including Suknachari, Chichingchera and Nabinchera. At Tushitpuri Bana Vihar in Nabinchera, they requested the Chakma people to exhibit their art of weaving which is an indispensable part of Maha Kathin Chibar Daan festival every year, as this art of weaving was not known to the people in Sri Lanka. So, although the time was not for Kathin Chibar Daan, a special show had to be arranged for them. In fact, they expressed willingness to replicate the art in their land, if possible.

Not only this, laymen are equally showing more and more interest to re-construct the link snapped by political reasons. Nowadays, many Chakmas, apart from those lay devotees accompanying Buddhist monks from Bangladesh, are making visits to Tripura, Arunachal Pradesh and Mizoram, some with the aim of visiting their relatives, some to have a glimpse of cultural attributes across the border. Cultural troupes are such groups who come to India to explore and exchange cultural attributes, especially during Bijhu festival, or on the pretext of attending conferences. At the same time, many Chakmas from India are visiting Bangladesh to see their relatives left behind in the past or to go on pilgrimage since there are lots of favoured Buddhist monasteries in Bangladesh.

Over the years the purview of pilgrimage for the Chakmas has expanded to great extent with many Chakmas taking up pilgrimage abroad. Due to technological and communication-related developments rapport with other Buddhist communities has developed as well as a new wave of inspiration and courage has been born out of cross-border exchanges. Not only the *bhikkhus* are taking such big steps, but the lay devotees are venturing into Sri Lanka, Thailand, Myanmar, etc. for the purpose of pilgrimage. And the efficacy of these holy trips has already been proved, as corroborated by many Chakma Buddhists. This is a kind of psychological impact of visiting a religious place — some pilgrims who were not keen believers of Buddhist rituals have come to believe in rituals after taking such pilgrimage.

In recent years, there have been certain voyages to Myanmar taken by the Chakmas from Tripura and Bangladesh bringing about new revelations to the fore. Some Buddhist monks from India and Bangladesh are in Myanmar pursuing Buddhist studies that focus on Tripitaka. They are in touch with local Chakmas of Myanmar, although who themselves know more identify as 'Chakmas' officially. They are locally known as 'Dainak'. They have their own Buddhist institutions and creolised cultural heritage now. Their pattern of dressing, food, language, everything has undergone change but still to some extent the ethnic thread has remained intact with certain commonalities. And whenever there are voyages by the Chakmas from India or Bangladesh, these transformed Chakmas of Myanmar experience ecstatical moments. Our recent trip to Yangon (October 2018) asserted this aspect of the lost thread under re-construction again. The hospitality and spontaneous service extended by the Chakmas of Myanmar was nothing but a gesture of ethnic solidarity beyond borders.

Conclusion

It seems the ice has been broken. The flow of cross-border exchanges involving Chakmas that started in a limited fashion will continue to grow in the coming days. Today's Tripura is a kind of tapestry of multi-cultural components. At this point, the plural social fabric of Tripura is ready to accommodate alien ideas and exchange indigenous heritage and culture with the outside world. However, the struggle for preserving own identity remains active under the belt. On the other hand, the Chakmas of Arunachal Pradesh seem to be more confident and content at the turning of events after passing through long years of ordeal. Hopeful of getting citizenship today or tomorrow, they are striving to prove their worth in different economic fields — a keen observer of the Chakma people living in Arunachal Pradesh or their lifestyle and those in other states of India could discern the difference. Perhaps it is the circumstances that mould a soul. Or, following Bourdieu, we can conclude that it is the result of the dialectic between the *habitus* and the *field*. Here I have tried to give a micro-perspective on how ethnicities are 'in an endless process of transformation' in the face of which the Chakma-Buddhists 'contest, revive, create, negotiate and re-negotiate' their ethnic identity.

Note

1. This is an extensively revised and updated version of Chakma, Rita. 2013. 'Relations Beyond Boundaries', *Eastern Quarterly*, 9(I&II), Spring & Monsoon, 5-15.

References

Adnan, Shapan. 2008. 'Contestations regarding identity, nationalism and citizenship during the struggles of the indigenous peoples of the Chittagong Hill Tracts of Bangladesh,' *International Review of Modern Sociology*, 34(1) (Spring), 27-45.

Asian Centre for Human Rights. 2015. Arunachal Pradesh – not the Chakmas/ Hajongs but other non-tribals pose bigger threat to indigenous peoples. New Delhi: Asian Centre for Human Rights, November 26.

Berger, Peter L. 1990. *The Sacred Canopy*. New York: Anchor Books.

Chakma, D.K., n.d., (ed.). *The Partition and the Chakmas*. Chennai: D.K. Chakma.

Grenfell, Michael, (ed.). 2012. Societal formation of the Chakmas: A tribe in Mizoram in North East India. New Delhi: Rawat Publications.

Oommen, T.K., 2002. *Pluralism, Equality and Identity*. New Delhi: Oxford University Press.

Prasad, Chunnu. 2006. 'Migration and the question of citizenship: People of Chittagong Hill Tracts in Arunachal Pradesh', *The Indian Journal of Political Science*, 67(3), (July-Sept), 471-490.

Said, Edward, 1977. *The Orientalism*. London: Penguin Books.

Singh, Deepak K., 2010. *Stateless in South Asia — The Chakmas between Bangladesh and India*. New Delhi: SAGE Publications India Pvt. Ltd.

Weber, Max. 1968. *The Protestant* Ethic and the Spirit of Capitalism (9th ed.). London: Unwin University Books.

6

Migration from Bihar to Assam and Sikkim

Sneha Mishra

The internal migration involving large numbers of people has large implication on the economy as a whole, both on the sending and receiving places. Bihar's rural populace continue to be dependent on the agricultural sector with high underemployment rate as compared to the national average. Out-migration is one of their livelihood alternatives available and the country's northeastern region particularly Assam and Sikkim is found to be their preferred destinations. Relying on both primary and secondary data, the study finds out the reasons, other than the economic factors, behind informal labour migration from Bihar to Assam and Sikkim and explores the preference of the migrants between the conflict-affected place (Assam in this case) and a peaceful place (Sikkim in this case) on the decision of labour migration from Bihar.

The primary motive of migration is monetary gains/economic benefits. A sizeable income difference between origin and destination places can reduce the negative influence of the distance between them which can be a significant intervening obstacle for migration (Barnum and Sabot, 1975; Lipton, 1980). Several other studies too have highlighted 'economic gain' as the main motive behind migration (Shields and Shields, 1989). Other studies have also discussed rural-urban migration where again the rural-urban income difference plays a significant role in making people migrate (Todaro, 1969; Todaro and Maruszko,1987). Lee (1966) credited to the push and pull factors for people's migration to different destinations. The push and pull factors are summarised in the following factors: factors associated with the place of origin, the place of destination, the intervening obstacles, and personal factors. For Lee, the push and pull factors are driving forces that can either induce people to migrate to new places or oblige them to leave old places. The push-pull factors can be economic, political, cultural and environmental in nature. A large number of studies have applied the push-pull framework and it is believed that various factors like demographic, economic and environmental are responsible for determining migration decisions. At first, it is the rural population growth that causes pressure on natural and agricultural resources which tends to force people to move out of the rural areas, and second is the economic reason in which higher wage acted as the major pull factor (Fields, 1975). The reasons behind in-migration and out-migration need to be understood, both at the place of origin and at the place of destination. In short, the reasons behind migration are so much mixed up that the migrant himself/herself is uncertain about the factors responsible for his/her migration. A combination of push and pull factors work simultaneously (Weissmann, 1965).

Bihar is one of the least-developed states of the country but the state has embarked upon a high growth rate in recent years. The state ranks twelfth in terms of geographical area but demographically it ranks third in the country. After separation from the undivided Bihar, it retained 75 per cent of the total populace and around 50 per cent of the natural resources. Between 2001 and 2011, Bihar has seen high decadal population growth of 25.42 per cent compared to the national average which was 17.64 per cent. The state tends to have a high proportion of the rural population with high poverty ratio. A number of human development indicators are still low just like the demographic indicators (sex ratio of 916 and female literacy rate at 42.73 per cent). In the Table 6.1, different demographic indicators are indicated.

The rural population of Bihar primarily depends on agriculture including other farm activities like fishery, livestock rearing and other non-farm activities. The MGNREGA programme (Mahatma Gandhi National Rural Employment Guarantee Act) which has succeeded in generating employment to many people has failed to get momentum in the state as there are several problems, most notably the delayed payments. On an average, just 33.82 days of employment per household could be generated which is one of the lowest in the country. The scarce resources along with restricted industrial growth have led to high unemployment which ultimately led to out-migration. A World Bank report maintained that in rural Bihar, the poor people and peasants have very limited livelihood options due to lack of land ownership, lack of education and social

Table 6.1: Indicators for Bihar

Demographic Variables	*2011*	*2001*	*Growth over the decade (%)*
Population	10.41 Cr*	8.30 Cr	25.42
Male	5.42 Cr	4.32 Cr	25.51
Female	4.98 Cr	3.97 Cr	25.32
Population growth	25.42%	28.43%	
Percentage of total population	8.60%	8.07%	
Sex ratio	918	919	
Density/km^2	1,106	881	25.53
Area (km^2)	94,163	94,163	
Literacy	61.80%	47.00%	31.48
Male literacy	71.20%	59.68%	19.30
Female literacy	51.50%	33.12%	55.49
Total literate	5.25 Cr	3.11 Cr	68.77
Male literate	3.16 Cr	2.06 Cr	53.10
Female literate	2.08 Cr	1.04 Cr	99.67

Note: * figures are in Crore
Source: Census of India, 2001 and 2011.

discrimination (World Bank, 2000). Under such circumstances, out-migration is a very crucial strategy for survival for the poor. Official records have shown that Bihar has recorded the highest rate of gross inter-state out-migration in the country (National Sample Survey Office, 2010).

Understandably, the rural population of the state is dependent upon agriculture and allied activities, and the underemployment rate is quite high as compared to the national average. Sharma (1995) has discussed the lack of economic diversification in rural Bihar. There is a very high shortage of non-farm employment opportunities for them. Thus, the surplus labours of the state generate large out-migration to other states of the country.

Bihar's Out-migration Trend

We intend to understand the overall scenario of out-migration from Bihar to other states. There are two major sources of data on migration: Census operation and NSSO. The migration data in the paper is based on the Census 2001.

Table 6.2: Out-migration from Bihar to other States according to 2001 Census

(Number and percentage)

	Rural	*Urban*	*Total*
Male	2390 (6.2)	495 (10.6)	3049 (7.1)
Female	1711 (4.8)	381 (9.4)	2211 (5.6)
Total	4101 (5.5)	876 (10.1)	5261 (6.3)

Source: Census of India, 2001, D-2; Numbers are in thousand; Figures in parenthesis are percentage to absolute numbers

Table 6.2 shows the number of out-migrants (in thousands) from Bihar and their proportionate share of the total population of the state. We can see very high out-migrants of about 5.3 million who have already migrated to other states of the country. This constitutes about 6.3 per cent of the total population of the state. Males are more migratory than their female counterparts. As we can see 7.1 per cent of the total male population preferred to migrate compared to 5.6 per cent of their female counterparts. If we compare the number of urban male population to the rural male population, the volume of male migration from the rural areas is much higher than the urban male migration. More than 2.3 million males from rural Bihar have migrated to other states whereas only 0.495 million males from urban Bihar have migrated to other states according to the 2001 census.

States in Northeast India have become the preferred destination for a large number of migrants from the state. Majority of the migrants from Bihar are unskilled and menial workers. These migrant labourers can get a job easily compared to their native place where the livelihood options are limited. Thus, they are driven towards the region despite its poor infrastructure, poor transport facilities, law and order problems and poor living condition. It is also plausible that the jobs taken up by the Bihari migrants are the ones which the indigenous inhabitants are either unwilling to take up or do not have the skill for. Having understood the background, the present study tries to study different factors responsible for the migration of labourers from Bihar who are engaged in Northeast region's urban informal sector mainly as street vendors, roadside tea sellers, barbers, hawkers, other daily wage workers, etc.

The present study is based on primary survey data about the majority of labour migrants in the urban areas of Assam and Sikkim who migrated from the rural parts of Bihar. Using primary and secondary data, the study finds out the reasons, along with the economic factors behind the out-migration from Bihar to the northeastern states, especially to Assam and

Sikkim. The major research questions have been formulated as below:

1) What are the main reasons for labourers from Bihar to migrate to Assam and Sikkim?
2) Is there any disparity in determining migrants' choice of destination?

Methodology and Data

The study is based on secondary data obtained from the Census of India (1991 and 2001) and the primary survey conducted among migrant labourers from Bihar who are employed in the urban informal sector. The census data do not specify about the labour migrants employed in the informal sector, these just give the overall picture of migrants in total. Hence, to fulfil the research objectives and understand the labour group in the informal sector, we conducted primary survey on labour migrants with a pre-structured questionnaire which included a separate section on reasons for migration.

The fieldwork was conducted during April-October 2016 to fulfil objectives of the study. Three districts namely Tinsukia, Bongaigaon and Kokrajhar were selected from Assam. The selection of these districts is based on the concentration of labour migrants from Bihar as well as the intensity of the conflict in these districts since we are to explore the preference between the conflict-affected place (Assam) and peaceful state (Sikkim). In Sikkim, the labour migrants in East district considered since it is a major economic centre of the state. The sample unit in our survey are the migrant workers in the urban informal sector. The urban informal sector in the study is defined as artisans, small business people who do not employ any labour, petty traders and non-agricultural casual workers in the informal sector. The casual workers may be the salaried workers under fixed employee or the daily wage workers with the employer not fixed, they work and get paid according to the availability of work (Sengupta, 2009). For example, we noticed that there are many retail store owners in Assam and Sikkim who employ Bihari migrants for loading and unloading works. Some labourers are more or less permanently engaged in a particular retail store, while some others work in different places and get paid accordingly. Hence, they do not have fixed employers.

We employed snowball sampling technique in order to locate the target, apart from this we took the help of the local people to find where the migrant workers work and the places where they live. We interviewed them by visiting them either in work sites or residence whichever they found convenient. The sample consisted of altogether 350 workers, out of which 200 are from Assam and 150 are from Sikkim. The migrants in Assam were 'little' apprehensive during the interview primarily because most of them have faced or heard of the several incidences of violence unleashed against the Biharis in the past. On the other side, it was easier to conduct interviews in Sikkim.

Reasons behind Migration

In the Indian census, the question on reasons for migration was introduced for the first time in 1981 by 'place of the last residence'. The same list of reasons continued in 1991 and 2001censuses except for the reason 'business' which was added in 1991 and the reason 'natural calamities' was dropped from the list in 2001. The reason 'moved after birth' was added in the 2001. Thus, the reasons for migration are categorised under the following: employment, business, education, marriage, moved after birth, the family moved and others. The Census of India defines migrants by place of birth and another is by place of last residence. The Census defines migrant by place of last residence as a person whose place of enumeration during the census is different than the place of immediate last residence (*see* Migration Data, Census of India, 2001).

The census data describes the homogeneity and heterogeneity of population living in an area. In this study migrants by the 'last place of residence' have been applied in order to give a more accurate picture and to better understand the migration scenario. Among the inter-state migrants in Assam, the migrants coming from Bihar outnumbered the migrants from other states which clearly specify the intensity of migration from Bihar in Assam. From the population census of 1991, of the total inter-state migrants, 34.90 per cent hailed from Bihar. The same holds true in 2001 as well which accounted for 31.29 per cent among the total inter-state migrants. For Sikkim, migrants from Bihar constituted the second highest with 23.55 per cent and 22.93 per cent of the total inter-state migrants in 1991 and 2001, respectively.

From Table 6.3, in the case of Assam, we found that the reason 'family moved' has been reported the most followed by 'business' and 'marriage'. The fourth most rated reason is unemployment. The scenario changes in the next census. 'Business' became the most rated reason in the next decade.

Table 6.3: Reasons for Migration

Reasons	*Assam*		*Sikkim*	
	1991	2001	1991	2001
Employment	18.92	18.7	27	34.11
Business	20.41	24.29	23.81	12.58
Education	0.65	0.49	1.99	1.12
Marriage	19.33	15.17	13.33	13.93
Moved after birth	0	1.22	0	1.68
Family moved	23.03	20.07	22.45	18.03
Others	17.65	20.07	11.41	18.56
Total	100	100	100	100.00

Source: Compiled from Census of India, 1991 and 2001; Numbers are in thousand.

So we see how there is a change in the reason behind migration for Bihari migration into Assam. The second most prominent reason is 'family moved' followed by the 'business'. On the other hand, in Sikkim, for census 1991, the economic/financial factors dominate. The two most prominent reasons rated by the respondents are 'employment' and 'business' followed by 'family moved'. The factor 'employment' still dominates in the census of 2001. However 'business' ranks after 'family moved'. We see that in both the censuses and for both the states 'marriage' is one of the prominent reasons, the reason behind this can be the female migration which follows after their marriage. Since the reasons are not gendered specific, it represents an overall scenario. There may be changes if we look at the reasons specifically for male and female.

Primary Data and Analysis

A total of 350 migrants were surveyed with a pre-structured questionnaire. Among them, 200 were from Assam and 150 were from Sikkim.

Table 6.4 represents the summary statistics of the surveyed migrants. The average age of Bihari migrants in Assam is 32.03 years whereas it is 29.17 years in Sikkim. We observe that the average age of migrants belongs to the working population which is 15-59 years. The mean working hours in a day are 9.76 and 10.43 hours for Assam and Sikkim respectively. The average years of migration are reported to 7.66 years for Assam and 8.07 years for Sikkim. The average expenditure, savings and income in Sikkim is comparatively higher than Assam. In both the states, the average number of dependent family members is 5.90 and 5.57 in Assam and Sikkim respectively. Likewise, few other variables are also mentioned in the Table 6.4.

Table 6.4: Summary Statistics of the Respondents from Bihar in Assam and Sikkim

State		*Mean*	*Minimum*	*Maximum*	*Median*	*Sd^*
Assam	Age	32.03	12.00	72.00	30.00	10.15
	Number of hours of work	9.76	3.00	14.00	10.00	1.96
	Years of migration	7.66	0.08	25.00	7.00	6.10
	Total expenditure	6941.90	0.00	24400.00	6600.00	3568.18
	Savings	5230.50	0.00	20000.00	5000.00	2687.29
	Income	12172.40	2100.00	29500.00	11350.00	4733.00
	Number of working members in the family	0.50	0.00	3.00	0.00	0.71
	Total dependent family members	5.90	2.00	11.00	6.00	1.67
	Number of children	2.73	0.00	8.00	3.00	1.51
Sikkim	Age	29.17	10.00	60.00	28.00	10.58
	Number of hours of work	10.93	6.00	14.00	12.00	1.84
	Years of migration	8.07	0.08	25.00	6.00	6.83
	Total expenditure	8188.36	0.00	27600.00	6850.00	6477.88
	Savings	5421.33	0.00	25000.00	5000.00	3573.72
	Income	13609.69	2000.00	48500.00	12500.00	7637.85
	Number of working members in the family	0.62	0.00	4.00	0.00	0.76
	Total dependent family members	5.57	2.00	12.00	5.00	1.68
	Number of children	2.53	0.00	6.00	2.00	1.34

Source: Primary survey data; ^- represents Standard deviation

Landlessness, conflicts in the family, social network at destination place (presence of friends and relatives who help them to settle initially and get a job), unemployment, the absence of desired employment opportunities, attraction towards city life, and loss of own business are a few of the reasons for migration (Mazumdar, 1960). There are several reasons for the migration of labourers from Bihar to Assam and Sikkim. The respondents were asked to give three priorities in order of preference. After giving weight to these priorities, the total weighted score was calculated on the basis of which the final rank order was drawn. This was done for Assam and Sikkim separately as well as combined to see the final ranks for different reasons (*see* Table 6.5).

For Assam, the first most important reason for migration is 'unemployment/jobless' in the native place as expected. The second is the economic reason that is 'financial crisis at home'. The third most important reason in order of priority is 'friends and relatives/social networks' at the

Table 6.5: Labour Migrants from Bihar to Assam

Reasons for Migrating to Destination	*1st Priority*	*Weighted Score*	*2nd Priority*	*Weighted Score*	*3rd Priority*	*Weighted Score*	*Total Weighted Score*
Landlessness at home	24	72	9	18	4	4	94
Joblessness	85	255	24	48	1	1	304
Financial constraint at native	32	96	84	168	35	35	299
Inadequate income in the previous occupation	30	90	26	52	5	5	147
For higher social status	3	9	10	20	12	12	41
Impressed by the city life	4	12	10	20	9	9	41
Friends and relatives/ social network	18	54	36	72	55	55	181
Others 1 (pull factors—good weather, nearby home)	0	0	0	0	2	2	4
Others 2 (push factors—natural calamities (flood, dry), family conflict, conflict with people in the neighbourhood, village)	4	12	1	2	7	7	14

Source: From primary survey data.

destination followed by 'inadequate income in the previous occupation'. 'Landlessness at home' also seems to be one of the significant reasons in order of priority. Rest all other reasons like 'for higher social status', 'impressed by the city life' and other push and pull factors do not seem to be of much significance (*see* Table 6.6).

For Sikkim, the reason in terms of order of priority shows that 'financial crisis at home' is the most important factor followed by 'jobless at home' which is the reverse if compared with Assam. The third foremost important reason is 'friends and relatives/social network' which is similar to Assam. 'Inadequate income in the previous occupation' ranks at fourth in order of priority. 'Landlessness' is the fifth in order of priority. In a similar manner like Assam, other reasons like 'for higher social status', 'impressed by the city life' and other push and pull factors do not seem to be of much significance.

Table 6.6: Labour Migrants from Bihar to Sikkim

Reasons for Migrating to Destination	*1st Priority*	*Weighted Score*	*2nd Priority*	*Weighted Score*	*3rd Priority*	*Weighted Score*	*Total Weighted Score*
Landlessness at home	12	36	8	16	1	1	53
Joblessness	46	138	15	30	1	1	169
Financial constraint at native	36	108	38	76	15	15	199
Inadequate income in the previous occupation	20	60	16	32	7	7	99
For higher social status	3	9	12	24	17	17	50
Impressed by the city life	2	6	16	32	15	15	53
Friends and relatives/ social network	20	60	31	62	26	26	148
Others 1 (pull factors— good weather, nearby home)	5	15	2	4	2	2	21
Others 2 (push factors — natural calamities (flood, dry), family conflict, conflict with people in the neighbourhood, village)	6	18	7	14	4	4	21

Source: From primary survey data.

Conclusion

The present study tries to find out the factors responsible for the migration of Bihar to Assam and Sikkim. At the time of the fieldwork, the migrants were asked about the factors responsible for their migration and asked to mention in the order of priority. It can be concluded that basically, the push factors from native/origin place are majorly responsible for the migration of the Bihari labour migrants. The study reveals that economic reason is the most prominent reason for migration from Bihar to Assam and Sikkim. Both joblessness and financial crisis at home were rated by most of the migrants in both the states. On comparing these two states, financial crisis is most rated in Sikkim and unemployment is most rated in Assam. The third most rated factor in both states is the presence of friends and relatives/ social networks at the destination that plays a very important role for the individual migrants. The presence of friends, relatives and villagers helps them in settling in a new place along with that their network helps them acquire a job in the new place. Another most prominent reason for migration is again related to the economic dimension that is the inadequate income in the previous occupation. The rural populace of Bihar are dependent for their livelihood on agriculture and allied activities but poverty and landlessness may bring about economic and even physical insecurity of the people hence pushing them to move to any new destination where they can earn their livelihood. Landlessness is the fifth most rated in the order of priority. So far we have discussed the various motivating reasons in the migration of labourers. However; these factors vary from person to person. Economic factors have generally predominated in migration in the study. The specific labour conditions in Bihar make the outflow of the population inevitable but its destination depends on several factors.

References

Barnum, H.N. and Sabot, R.H. 1975. *Migration, education and urban surplus labor*. Paris: OECD Development Center, Employment Series.

Census of India, 2001. *Migration Tables-D series*. New Delhi: Registrar General and Census Commissioner of India.

Census of India, 2011. *Migration Tables-D series*. New Delhi: Registrar General and Census Commissioner of India.

Fields, G. 1975. 'Rural-urban migration, urban unemployment and underemployment, and job search activity in LDC's,' *Journal of Development Economics* 2(2), 165-88.

Lee, E. 1966. 'A Theory of Migration', *Demography* 3(1), 47-57.

Lipton, M. 1980. 'Migration from rural areas of poor countries: The impact on rural productivity and income distribution', *World Development*, 8(1), 1-24.

Mazumdar, D.N. 1960. *Social Contours of an Industrial City*. Bombay: Asia Publishing House, 63.

National Sample Survey Office. 2010. *Migration in India 2007-2008, NSS 64th round July 2007-June 2008*. New Delhi: Ministry of Statistics and Programme Implementation, Government of India.

Sengupta, A.K. 2009. 'The Challenge of Employment in India: An Informal Economy Perspective', *Report of the National Commission for Enterprises in the Unorganised Sector, Government of India*, Volumes 1 and 2. New Delhi: Academic Foundation.

Sharma A.N. 1995. 'Political Economy of Poverty in Bihar', *Economic and Political Weekly*, 30(41/42), October 14-21, 2587–2589.

Shields, G. & Shields, M. 1989. 'The emergence of migration theory and a suggested new direction', *Journal of Economic Surveys*, 3, 277-304.

Todaro, M.P. 1969. 'A model of labor migration and urban unemployment in less-developed countries', *American Economic Review* 59, 138-48.

Todaro, M.P. & Maruszko, L. 1987. 'Illegal migration and US immigration reform: A conceptual framework', *Population and Development Review*13, 101-14.

Weissmann, E. 1965. 'The Urban Crisis in the World', *Urban Affairs Quarterly* 1(1), 414.

World Bank. 2000. Development Challenges and Poverty in Bihar: Towards a Development Strategy, World Bank.

7

Youths Migration from 'Paradise Unexplored'

An Indispensable Journey

K.N. Tennyson

Northeast India is a multi-religious, multi-linguistic, multi-culture and multi-ethnic society. It is called the land of jewels, land of rising sun, one-horned rhinoceros and festival of festivals, and is also the region where the British fought several battles. Another important feature of the region is that it is the gateway to Southeast Asia. However, due to difficult connectivity and geographical isolation, underdevelopment, economic backwardness and law and order problem, the region remains one of the most unexplored regions in the country.

Imbroglio Northeast India

Ever since India came into existence, Indian policy-makers deem the Northeast India region as disturbed area, and thus the Armed Forces (Special Powers) Act, 1958 was promulgated by the first President of India, Rajendra Prasad on May 22, 1958.[1] The implicit reason why the Act was imposed in the region was that of the Nagas refusal to join the Union of India and declared their independence on August 14, 1947, along with Pakistan after the partition of the Indian subcontinent. Further, on May 16, 1951, the Nagas led by the Naga National Council (NNC) conducted a plebiscite wherein 99.99 per cent of the Nagas were reported to have voted 'in favour of independence from India' (Vashum, 2005). Nonetheless, Indian leaders did not bow down by the rebellious nature of the Nagas, and used various diplomatic means, including the visit of India's first Prime Minister Jawaharlal Nehru to Kohima (the present state's capital of Nagaland) along with Burma (now Myanmar) Prime Minister U Nu in

March 1953 to 'convince the Naga people that their progress and prosperity lay with India' (Zhimoni, 2004) but, even Nehru could not win over the Nagas. The Naga nationalist leaders argued the Nagas were never under any external powers even during the British period and 'insisted on full sovereignty from India'. On June 18, 2005, Th. Muivah, the General Secretary of the National Socialist Council of Nagalim (NSCN-IM) reiterating Naga's right to self-determination told Shekhar Gupta, *on* NDTV 24×7's *Walk the Talk* programme, 'Nagas and Nagaland were never conquered by an alien nation, including India'.[2]

Following the Nagas, various other indigenous communities of the region too began to revolt against New Delhi, thus, the hope for peace was derailed even before most of the Northeast Indian states came into existence. Prakash Singh, a retired veteran police officer, who had worked in close association with the people of the region narrating the inspirational role that the Nagas played in the insurgent movement in the Northeast region wrote, 'The Naga insurgent has been some kind of a role model for separatist movements in other areas of the Northeast' (Singh, 2010).

AFSPA ('a draconian law') was introduced in the region to curb violence and internal disturbances (insurgent movement), but peace still remains elusive. Today, as a result of the law and order problems and the dim prospect of an economic return to the investors, no outside investors are willing to invest in the region, thus, the region continues to remain industrially underdeveloped and economically poor. However, underdevelopment and isolation is not a new development for the people of the region. Even during the British period, the British followed a policy of non-interference and kept the most part of the region isolated from the rest of the country. The reason being that the British did not find interesting to rule over the geographically isolated, economically poor and areas inhabited by the 'hostile' tribes, such as the Nagas. Lord Dalhousie, the then Governor-General of India (1848-1856) expressing one such view said,

> ... Our possession (of the region) could bring no profit to us, and would be as costly to us as it would be unproductive ... advantage ... be obtained by refraining from all seizuer of the territory of these Nagas, and by confining ourselves to be the establishment of effective means of defence on the line of our own frontiers (quoted in Shimray, 2005).

In light of this background, the British imposed the Bengal Eastern Frontier Regulation, 1873. The regulation prohibited outsiders 'from going' into places such as the district of Kamrup, Darrang, Nowgong, Sibsagar, Lakhimpur (Garo Hills), Khasi and Jaintia Hills, Naga Hills and Cachar 'without a pass' (inner line permit) issued by the chief executive.[3] The consequence of such policy was the complete isolation of the region from the rest of the world. The British argued that the inner line permit was necessary for maintaining peace and governance, but, such law 'creates a barrier' between the people of the Northeast region and other parts of the country. It is because of such a divisive policy, most of the people of the region do not feel the sense of belonging to the Indian national identity.

Development Challenges in Northeast India

Like the British, future policy-makers too did not take much interest in the development of the region until the then Prime Minister P.V. Narasimha Rao (June 21, 1991- May 16, 1996) introduced the Look East policy. V.I.K. Sarin, a veteran journalist who reported from the region during the worst period of the insurgent movement, wrote, 'The (Northeast) region remained virtually neglected until the Chinese invasion of 1962'. He further added, 'Although large investments have been made for the development of the area in the post-1962 period, the region remains economically backwards' (Sarin, 1980). The Chinese invasion indeed opened the eyes of the policy-makers towards the importance of developing the Northeast region, but it was only after the shift of India's foreign policy towards Southeast Asia, New Delhi began to vigorously strive to integrate the once forgotten and neglected region with the country's development programme. The Indian government was compelled to develop this region because the success of the Look East policy and now the Act East policy lays in better connectivity of the Northeast region with Southeast Asia.

In a sharp departure from New Delhi earlier policy of keeping the Northeast India region undeveloped, former Prime Minister, Manmohan Singh emphasised on the need to develop the region. Speaking at the releasing function of the *North Eastern Region Vision 2020* document in New Delhi on July 2, 2008, he remarked, 'The North-Eastern region is the land of the rising sun for India. The time has come for the sun to shine on it and shine brightly'. He further added, his 'government has made connectivity and infrastructure development the cornerstone of regional development in the Northeast'.[4] Prime Minister Narendra Modi, the successor of Manmohan Singh, too highlighted the need for the development of the region and said, 'India's growth story shall never be complete until the [North] eastern part [of India] progresses at par with the western part. The Northeast can be the New Engine of India's growth'. He added the policy-makers 'are addressing the special needs of the Northeast region to enable growth parity with the rest of the country'.[5]

The changing attitude of the Indian leaders towards Northeast India is a welcome development. But the problems remain. In some places of the region, the non-state actors are running parallel governments. They directly take commission from government projects and at the same time collect tax from villagers, government employees, businessmen and contractors (*see* Sinha, 2007), thus, creating serious policy problems and development challenges. The arrest of a new unknown militant group United Kuki National Army (UKNA) at Boljol village, Churachandpur district, Manipur, on February 3, 2018, by the police for demanding a sum of Rs. 50 lakhs from the Autonomous Development Council, Churachandpur is a manifestation to this point.[6] Sadly, it's not only the public but, at times, even educational institutions too suffered from the tyranny of the militants. There are many instances where the educational institutions in the region, particularly in Manipur, could not function smoothly because of the interference (threat) by the militants.[7]

What hurts the people of the region, especially the youth, the most is that they not only suffered at the hand of the non-state actors but also from the high-handedness of the security forces of the country. Taking advantage of the 'special powers' empowered to them, the security forces suppressed the rights and liberties of the civilians and had also targeted religious places and educational institutions. The Global Coalition to Protect Education from Attack in its *Education under Attack 2014* report stated that during 2010, as many as "129 schools were used as barracks or bases across the country, particularly in Bihar, Chhattisgarh and Jharkhand, but also in the country's northeast, in Tripura, Manipur, Nagaland and Assam, (thus,) disrupting education for an estimated 20,800 students".[8]

Another contagious issue that is crippling the society of the region is the problem of corruption. Corruption is deeply engrossed in the life of the people that it's 'no longer considered a taboo'. The politicians, bureaucrats and contractors, the curators of development, instead of utilising the developmental fund for development activities joined hands with the insurgent and skim-off developmental funds into their coffer. Shashi Shekhar, the Editor-in-Chief of the *Hindustan Times* relating the unholy alliance between the separatist and policymakers of the region wrote,

> While travelling through the remote areas of Manipur and Nagaland in the 1990s, I discovered that billions of rupees allotted by the Centre were not utilised for development; instead, they lined the pockets of bureaucrats and politicians. Rather than stopping them, the local police and paramilitary personnel were in cahoots with the corrupt. Clearly, when it comes to profit and loss, guns don't differentiate between separatist groups and those in uniform.[9]

Since there is no development there are no alternative job opportunities for the youth, save government job. But, getting into government service is a distant dream for the majority of the youth, because, government jobs have been so commercialised that it belongs to those who are politically connected and have the financial power and not for the poor and deserving. The recent discovery (November, 2017) of the long-hidden 'cash-for-job scam' in the Assam Public Service Commission by the Assam police is one such perfect example.[10] As corruption in society increased, the number of educated unemployment also increased, which, inadvertently compelled many disgruntled youth to either take up arms or migrate to metropolitan cities in search of jobs and livelihood.

Youth and Employment

'Employment generation is the key channel through which economic growth translates into prosperity for the population', highlighted the Government of India, Ministry of Labour and Employment report. It further added, 'In a growing economy, employment growth with rising productivity is the most effective mechanism available to the poor to participate in the growth process and raise their standard of living' (Government of India, 2016). But, on the contrary, the employment opportunities in the Northeast region are in a bad state of affairs. The Ministry of Labour and Employment, *Fifth Annual Employment-Unemployment Survey (2015-16)* shows that Tripura recorded the highest unemployment rate in the country (19.7%) followed by Sikkim (18.1%). While Mizoram and Meghalaya have done relatively well with only 3.0 per cent and 4.8 per cent unemployed respectively, the other states of the region are far above the all India level of 5 per cent, with Arunachal Pradesh recording 8.9 per cent, Nagaland - 8.5 per cent, Assam - 6.1 per cent and

Manipur - 5.7 per cent (Government of India, 2016). The official statistics indicating the demand and supply for job in the region too display a gloomy picture, with states like Arunachal Pradesh and Manipur recording zero (0) per cent placement in 2014 (Table 7.1). Interestingly, Tripura, which has the highest unemployment rate in the country, is reported to have had the highest percentage of 'placement to submission ratio' among the northeastern states (Table 7.1).

Table 7.1: Employment Exchange Statistics (All categories) Northeast State wise 2014

State	*Employment Exchanges/ UEIGBs $*	*(in Thousands)*					*% of live register to total live register*	*% of placement to submission*
		Registration	*Vacancies notified*	*Submission*	*Placements*	*Live registration $*		
Arunachal Pradesh	11	3.1	0.0	0.0	0.0	57.2	0.1	0.0
Assam	52	269.3	4.0	32.3	1.1	1826.9	3.8	3.5
Manipur	11	17.5	1.2	29.9	0.0	712.1	1.5	0.0
Meghalaya	12	6.2	0.2	1.3	0.0	37.6	0.1	2.1
Mizoram	3	3.9	0.3	2.9	0.1	29.6	0.1	2.3
Nagaland	8.13	0 0	0 0	0 0	0 0	64.1	0.1	3.4
Sikkim*								
Tripura	5	30.5	0.1	4.1	2.4	595.6	1.2	59.4

Notes: * No Exchange is working in the State.
$ At the end of the year.
Total may not tally due to rounding off.

Source: Abstract from Government of India, Ministry of Labour and Employment, *Employment Exchange Statistics*, 2015. New Delhi: Directorate General of Employment and Training, 2015, 28.

Unemployment is a global phenomenon, but the problems in the country augmented when the majority of the youth are unemployed. The same holds true for the Northeast region. Brigadier Sushil Kumar Sharma, a veteran military officer argued that 'the core insurgent ideology has gradually given way to practical economic interests, especially among the younger generation', which in turn help in 'substantial changes in their security environment' in other northeastern states, but, not in Manipur. The reason why insurgents continue to flourish in Manipur according to him is '[t]he lure of easy money and lack of employment opportunities' in the state (Sharma, 2016).

There are various reports which point out the existence of a large number of unemployed youth in the region (Table 7.2). This called for an

Table 7.2: Unemployment Rate (per 1000) of Youth (15-24 years) according to the Usual Principal Status Approach (ps) for Each Northeast State

Sl. No.	*Name of States*	*15-24 years*		
		Male	*Female*	*Person*
1.	Arunachal Pradesh	465	426	446
2.	Assam	174	412	220
3.	Manipur	51	181	79
4.	Meghalaya	112	163	132
5.	Mizoram	85	81	83
6.	Nagaland	166	258	199
7.	Sikkim	496	526	502
8.	Tripura	363	330	355
	All India	**163**	**244**	**181**

Source: Abstract from Government of India, Ministry of Labour and Employment, *Report on Youth Employment-Unemployment Scenario (2012-13)*, Volume III (Chandigarh: Labour Bureau, 2013), 7 (Table 7.3).

urgent need on the part of the policy-makers of the region to develop the feeble economy and create employment opportunities for the disgruntled youth. But, it will be a Herculean task to solve the problem, because, even the basic necessities of life such as safe drinking water, electricity and roads are in a pathetic condition in most places of the region.

Ironically, the region which recorded high unemployment rate in the country is also the region with some of the most literate states. The literacy rate in most states of the region, save Arunachal Pradesh and Assam, are much higher than the national level (Table 7.3). Nonetheless, this does not provide any solace to the youth of the region, because, more and more youth are going to be unemployed. This fact is clearly stated in the Indian Chamber of Commerce (ICC) and the Pricewaterhouse Coopers (PwC) study, which confirmed that Northeast India region 'will have only 2.6 million jobs. And half of this demand will be in Assam alone', but, the number of job-seekers will increase to 17 million in 2011-2022.[11]

The economic condition of the region is not better either. The region is mountainous and industrially underdeveloped where a large number of the population depends on agriculture for their livelihood. The official records indicated that in Nagaland and Meghalaya around 71.14 per cent (Government of Nagaland, 2016), and 70 per cent (Government of Meghalaya, 2009) of the population were directly or indirectly engaged in agriculture and allied sectors, whereas in Arunachal Pradesh, Sikkim and Manipur, it was about 63 per cent (Planning Commission, Government of

Table 7.3: Northeast States Literacy Rates in 2001 and 2011

State	*2001*	*2011*
Arunachal Pradesh	54.34	66.95
Assam	63.25	73.18
Manipur	69.93	79.85
Mizoram	88.80	91.58
Meghalaya	62.56	75.48
Nagaland	66.59	80.11
Sikkim	68.81	82.20
Tripura	73.19	87.75
All India	64.83	74.04

Source: Abstract from *Human Development Report of North East States, December 2011* (Government of India: Ministry of Development of North Eastern Region, 2011), 21-22.

India, 2009), 60 per cent (Government of Sikkim, 2015) and 52.81 per cent (Government of Manipur 2016), respectively. However, B.C. Barah, the former Principal Scientist at the National Centre for Agricultural Economics and Policy Research, ICAR New Delhi, wrote, 'Agriculture in the (Northeast) region has not been able to generate surpluses for investment and augment purchasing power' (Barah, 2006). Since the region is industrially underdeveloped and agricultural activities no longer remain attractive to the young generation, hundreds and thousands of youth are migrating to metropolitan cities in search of jobs and livelihood.

Interestingly, the people moving out from the region to other parts of the country are youth, unlike, that of the people coming from other parts of the country into the region, who are mostly elderly people (labourers and businessmen). The youth of the region like the youth of other undeveloped and economically poor region move out of their native place not by choice, but by compulsion. Fortunately, the youth of the region find no difficulty in getting part-time jobs in metropolitan cities as there is high demand for cheap labour. Dolly Kikon, a social anthropologist, opined that the northeasterners were preferred to other Indian youths because of "their 'un-Indian' looks, 'the exotic Asians,' and in association with this, their reputation for being hardworking and loyal".[12]

Yet, all is not well. The boys and girls from the region move out of their native places with much hope and expectation, but only to end up in pink collar jobs (sales, service and clerical jobs), where exploitation of workers is at the highest level. At the same time, once away from home, they face various hardships and difficulties, including in the worst form of 'racial discrimination' in one form or the other. Since, most of them belong to the Mongolian race and are different ethnically, physically and culturally from the rest of their compatriots (Indians) living in other parts of the country, others often had the misconception that they do not belong to the larger Indian community. This sad reality is the reflection of the image that was a portrait of the Northeast region to the outside world by media fraternity. Until recently, the news and visual impression that one received on the region was of the news and image of the insurgency (the fight between the Indian security forces and the insurgents), bandh, protest and political crisis. Hence, the people outside the region have only negative images of the people living in the Northeast region.

However, with India enthusiastically trying to rebuild its relations with Southeast Asia, the Northeast India region has become an important player in India's foreign policy. One such positive development is the establishment of the Ministry of Development of North Eastern Region (DoNER), the only region in the country to have a separate ministry. The said ministry is entrusted with the responsibility of planning, execution and monitoring of development projects in the region.[13] Today, the ministry not only aims to achieve its vision of accelerating development of the region but, is also playing a significant role in safeguarding the life and welfare of the North Easterners living in other parts of the country, especially in metropolitan cities. The ministry in collaboration with other departments and universities has constructed a number of hostels for northeastern students and working women in the national capital city, Delhi. The Rajiv Gandhi Hostel for Girls (RGHG) located at North Campus, University of Delhi and the working women's hostel located at Jasola, New Delhi are two such examples. There is also a proposal to set up more hostels for northeastern students in Jawaharlal Nehru University and Bangalore University.

Further, the central government is putting extra efforts to sensitise the police forces of different metropolitan cities to deal with crimes against people from Northeastern states.[14] As they are physical, culturally and ethnically different from the rest of their compatriots, most of them face the problems of discrimination in one form or the other. It was for this reason, Delhi police have launched the Special Police Unit for North East Region (SPUNER), and the Government of Karnataka and Haryana have appointment senior police officers as the nodal officers for northeasterners in Bangalore city, and Gurugram (formerly Gurgaon). The policy-makers of the three Indian states (Delhi, Karnataka and Haryana) are giving special attention to the problems and issues of the northeast people living in their states, because, a large number of crimes against the northeast people were reported from these states, especially from Delhi (Table 7.4). With the crime against them becoming a major political problem, the central government constituted a committee in 2014, under the Chairmanship of MP Bezbaruah to study the problems and difficulties faced by them living in other parts of the country, 'especially in the metropolitan areas, and to suggest suitable remedial measures which could be taken by the government'.[15]

Table 7.4: Crime against Northeast People[16]

Year	*Delhi*	*Bengaluru*	*Gurugram*
2012	55	18	0
2013	72	4	0
2014	286	7	9

Source: Press Information Bureau, Government of India, Ministry of Home Affairs (Lok Sabha Debate).

Delhi being the capital city, large numbers of the north-easterners live and work here, therefore, the central government was compelled to walk the extra mile and adopt various confidence-building measures between the northeast people and other communities. The appointment of 439 northeast youth into Delhi Police consciously is one such step aimed to bridge the communication gap between the people of the region and law enforcing agencies. Another major attraction that the Ministry of Tourism and DoNER initiated to create awareness about the region and to promote tourism in the region is the *North East festival*, showcasing the splendid cultural dance, dress, music and foods of the region.[17] The central government is organising such colourful carnival not only to create awareness about the natural beauty of the region and its people but, also aimed at inculcating a sense of belongingness and acceptability of the northeasterners into the larger Indian community.

Conclusion

Unlike in the past, the policies of the government towards Northeast India have witnessed positive change, so also is the attitude of other Indians towards the Northeast people. Even, the state governments of the region are beginning to realise the need for change and some have initiated confidence-building measures like the establishment of the Anti-Corruption Cell in the office of the Bharatiya Janata Party (BJP) led Chief

Minister of Manipur, N. Biren Singh in March 2017 to look into the complaints received from general public.[18] But, the central and state governments need to do much more if India really wants to make the region to be the heart of the Act East policy.[19]

What is disturbing about the region is that hundreds and thousands of youth are moving out of the region in search of jobs and livelihood. Prashant Jha, the Political Editor of the *Hindustan Times* pointing out the sad state of affairs wrote, the youth of the region 'looked wistfully at the pace of change and the scale of opportunities in the bigger cities, Delhi, Mumbai, Bengaluru, Pune. Many had studied in those places, some had even worked there, many more aspired to move to these centres. And all of it was because they felt their own states did not have the same opportunities'. This truth cannot be denied. Since the plans and policies initiated do not in any way benefit the youth, the youth of the region have lost trust on the machinery of the state government, and as a result, they are inadvertently compelled to move out to metropolitan cities.

This brings us to the conclusion that the policy-makers need to reassess their plans and policies and focus on good governance and development. People-oriented programme and corrupt-free state is the need of the hour. The governments of the region, therefore, need to espouse more confidence-building measures, such as controlling corruption and ensuring a merit-based appointment, so as to gain the confidence of its citizens, especially the youth. Without which, there can never be peace and stability in the region, and without peace and stability, development will never become a reality, no matter how good and effective the plan and policy of the government might be. Further, there is a need to evaluate the development programmes that are taking place in the region and create additional employment opportunities to tap the enormous human resources available in the region.

Notes

1. According to the Armed Forces (Special Powers) Act, 1958, "any commissioned officer, warrant officer, non-commissioned officer or any other person of equivalent rank in the armed forces may, in a disturbed area," "arrest, without warrant" any suspicious person or "use force, even to the causing of death," against any person.
2. *Walk the Talk* with Th. Muivah, General Secretary, National Socialist Council of Nagalim, June 18, 2005, p. 3; *Also see BBC Hardtalk* with Th. Muivah, General Secretary, National Socialist Council of Nagalim, April 29, 2005, p. 7.

3. Read the *Regulation 5 of 1873 (Bengal Eastern Frontier Regulation, 1873)*, 27 August 1873.
4. Former Prime Minister of India, Dr. Manmohan Singh, Speeches, 'PM releases North Eastern Region Vision 2020 Documents', New Delhi, July 2, 2008, http://archive pmo.nic.in/drmanmohansingh/speech-details.php?nodeid=670, (Accessed October 7, 2017).
5. Prime Minister's Office, 'English rendering of PM Modi's speech at the laying of the foundation stone of several projects to the nation in Manipur', March 16, 2018, http://pib.nic.in/PressReleaseIframePage.aspx? PRID=1524805, (Accessed March 21, 2018).
6. 'Ccpur police arrest one person of unknown UG group 'UKNA', *Imphal Free Press*, February 4, 2018, https://www.ifp.co.in/page/items/46672/ccpur-police-arrest-one-person-of-unknown-ug-group-ukna/, (Accessed May 3, 2018).
7. 'Killing the goose that lays the golden egg: Banning Catholic schools', *The Sangai Express*, February 9, 2018, http://www.thesangaiexpress.com/killing-goose-lays-golden-egg-banning-catholic-schools/, (Accessed March 6, 2018).
8. Global Coalition to Protect Education from Attack, *Education under Attack 2014*, 140.
9. Shashi Shekar, 'A dangerous disconnect in NE', *Hindustan Times*, March 5, 2018, 14.
10. Samudra Gupta Kashyap, 'Assam Jobs Scam: how Officers pass through APSC backdoor', *The Indian Express*, November 14, 2017, 13.
11. ICC & PwC India, India's North-East Diversifying Growth Opportunities, January 2013, p. 11, https://www.pwc.in/assets/pdfs/publications/2013/north-east_summit-2013.pdf, (Accessed February 14, 2018).
12. Dolly Kikon, 'Understanding Indigenous Migration in Northeast India', *The Morung Express*, November 30, 2016.
13. Ministry of Development of North Eastern Region, *About Ministry*, http://mdoner.gov.in/#, (Accessed August 9, 2018).
14. Sandali Tiwari, 'Northeast helpline gets 30 calls in just one day', *The Indian Express, Express Newline*, October 30, 2014, 1.
15. Press Information Bureau, Government of India, Ministry of Home Affairs, 'Bezbaruah Committee', December 22, 2015, http://pib.nic.in/newsite/PrintRelease. aspx?relid=133765, (Accessed June 14, 2018).
16. Press Information Bureau, Government of India, Ministry of Home Affairs, 'Crime against people from North-East', March 3, 2015, http://pib.nic.in/newsite/Print Release.aspx?relid=116314, (Accessed May 21, 2017).
17. *North East festival-Connecting People, Celebrating Life*, http://www.northeast festival.com/#about (Accessed January 5, 2018).
18. Government of Manipur, *Order regarding to establish an Anti-Corruption Cell in the Office of the Chief Minister, Manipur*, http://manipur.gov.in/?p=11915, (Accessed April 17, 2018).

19. Press Information Bureau, Government of India, Prime Minister's Office, 'Preliminary English rendering of PM's address at the inaugural session of Advantage Assam-Global Investors Summit 2018', Guwahati, Assam, February 3, 2018, http://pib.nic.in/newsite/PrintRelease.aspx?relid=176132, (Accessed April 17, 2018).

References

Barah, B.C. 2006. 'Agricultural Development in North-East India Challenges and Opportunities', *ICAR Policy Brief*, 25, December 1.

Government of Manipur. 2016. *Economic Survey, Manipur, 2015-16*. Imphal: Directorate of Economics and Statistics, p. vi.

Government of Meghalaya. 2009. *Meghalaya Human Development Report 2008*. Shillong: Planning Department, pp. 4, 10 & 120.

Government of Nagaland. 2016. *Nagaland State Human Development Report 2016*. Kohima: Department of Planning and Coordination.

Government of Sikkim. 2015. Sikkim Human Development Report 2014: Expanding Opportunities, Promoting Sustainability. New Delhi: Routledge.

Government of India. 2016. *Report on Fifth Annual Employment-Unemployment Survey (2015-16), Vol. I*. Chandigarh: Labour Bureau, Ministry of Labour & Employment.

Planning Commission, Government of India. 2009. *Arunachal Pradesh Development Report*. New Delhi: Academic Foundation.

Shimray, A.S. Atai. 2005. *Let Freedom Ring: Story of Naga Nationalism*. New Delhi: Promilla Publishers.

Sinha, S.P. 2007. Lost Opportunities: 50 Years of Insurgency in the North-East and India's Response. New Delhi: Lancer Publisher and Distributors.

Singh, Prakash. 2010. *Kohima to Kashmir: On the Terrorist Trail*. New Delhi: Rupa Publications.

Sharma, Sushil Kumar. 'Educated Unemployment and Insurgency in Manipur: Issues and Recommendations', *IDSA Policy Brief*, February 23.

Vashum, R. 2005. *Nagas' Right to Self-Determination*. New Delhi: Mittal Publications.

Zhimoni, Kuhoi K. 2004. *Politics and Militancy in Nagaland*. New Delhi: Deep & Deep Publications.

8

Migration from the Periphery

A Case Study of Manipuri Youth in Delhi

Huidrom Renuka

In the last two decades, large sections of youth from Northeast states have migrated to the metropolitan cities. Among the metropolitan cities, Delhi has been a particular favourite among them. Most of the youth, aspire for civil services stay in Delhi in order to prepare for it, or for higher education. Some also work in the new service sectors like shopping malls, restaurants, BPO sectors etc. Those migrated to Delhi live mostly inhabit in certain pockets of the city and some of them even begin small-scale business ventures like grocery store which sells edible ingredients used in cooking by people from the region, otherwise hard to find in a city like Delhi. Despite the fact that they face discrimination on racial grounds, they do not wish to move out of metropolitan spaces. Rather they live in specific localities which have a large number of people from the Northeast as its inhabitants since they feel that they will have someone to help them in case of crisis and problem.

The author highlights some of the emerging factors which lead people of Northeast in general and Manipuri youth, in particular, are made to migrate from their own places. Author also attempts to engage with two questions. One, why is there an increasing trend of migration among the youth of Northeast in particular of Manipur to Delhi in the last few decades? In continuation of this question, why is it that despite discrimination in metropolitan cities (specifically Delhi) the youth are still migrating? The conditions of youth negotiating with insecurities, and disappointment, living in Delhi are also looked into.

Migration is not a new phenomenon in the history of human civilisation. It is defined as the movement of people from one place to another across political boundaries. It is a sign of a wide range of disparities in economic, political and social conditions between different regions, places or countries. In countries like India, migration takes place mostly due to unemployment, displacement, natural calamities, and under-development at the place of origin. One can say that the main driving force behind migration is the expectation of a better standard of life. In most cases, youth driven by hope for better job prospects, good lifestyle and as an escape from the realities of life in their hometowns migrate to bigger cities. Historically, internal migration in India has been low (Davis 1961), and a declining trend in mobility is noticed until about the 1990s (Kundu and Gupta, 1996). The National Sample Survey data for 1992–1993 and 1999–2000 suggested an increase in mobility during the last decade (Srivastava and Sasikumar, 2003).

Each year young people from Northeast migrated to the metropolitan cities (*see* Marchang, 2011; Usha & Shimray, 2010; Ramesh, 2012; McDuie-Ra, 2013). Although no reliable statistical information is available regarding the exact demographic composition, it has been suggested that Delhi attracts the largest number of migrants, the majority of whom are young and single. Migration has become an important livelihood diversification strategy for many poor people everywhere, internal migration is an activity undertaken primarily by youth and it is on the rise in India as well.

According to the Economic Survey of Delhi (2012–2013), the percentage of migration in Delhi was 24.38 per cent in 2011. Census of India (2001) recorded that half of the Northeast migrants to Delhi are youth in the age group of 15-29 years. In the 2001 census, it has been recorded that 64 per cent of the youth from Manipur and Nagaland in the overall migration data from the Northeast states in Delhi only. People from the region in general and Manipur, in particular, choose the capital city as their main destination in compare with other major cities despite atrocities, injustices, discrimination and prejudices invariably. They continue to migrate to seek better prospect and avenues. Specifically, the youth from margin who lack in various resources want to explore better opportunities and city lifestyle. They see many avenues in the cities which they cannot find at home and they venture out for various activities which are not available in their home towns or villages from where they are coming.

Understanding the Process of Northeast migration in Delhi

Migration can be classified into three types starting from the early 1980s to the present day. In the first type of migration during the early 1980s people from the region used to migrate mostly for educational purposes. After acquiring their studies or degrees people went back to their hometowns as there was not much competition. The second type of migration started from the late 1990s, in this generational people from Northeast were engage in both employment as well as in education. After the completion of their studies, they looked for jobs, mostly engaging in term of professionals who are employed in various professions like teaching, nursing, doctor, etc. Those who work in government job and other private sector stay until their retirement and return to their states. The third type of migration relates to education, employment and mass migration in recent years. Within this, we can categories three groups of migration.

Youth come for higher education as Delhi offers the better education in the country, moreover, after completion of their higher education they sit for civil services examinations and many of them enrolled in coaching centres to prepare for competitive exams. There is another group of youth who are in professions like teaching, working in central government jobs, IT professions and doctors who stay in the city.

People who are from a very poor section of Northeast society mostly working in the retail shops, restaurants, shopping malls, beauty parlours with modest qualifications and many of the violence which happened to people of the region happens on them. Most migrants are in their 20s when they come to Delhi. Through fieldwork,[1] it is found that the trend of families migrating to Delhi together, especially from areas affected by conflict and development-induced displacement. When the youth migrate to the city they take help either from their friends or relatives who are already settled in the city. The recent finding also shows a picture of increasing mass migration including parents who belong to the above mentioned third category of migration. The respondent gave various reasons for leaving their hometown, including seeking refuge from ethnic conflicts, displacement due to state-led development projects, corruption, low levels of investment and unemployment which are emerging rapidly in northeast states particularly in Manipur.

Emerging push factor of Manipuri youth in Delhi

During the fieldwork, youth migrants gave various reasons for leaving Manipur including seeking refuge from ethnic conflict-torn villages, atrocities of paramilitary forces, and state-led displacement. However, most of them migrated because of the availability of work in retail, hospitality and call centres. Job opportunities are limited in the region due to a number of associated difficulties such as corruption, low level of investment, capital flight and the proliferation of illegal and semi-legal economies. Besides, seeking employment, the opportunity to study outside the Northeast region is a major impetus for youth migration (Duncan, 2012).

In the period after globalisation and economic liberalisation, many development projects have been implemented in the region with a mission of connecting with other Asian countries while opening the 'East Gate' as a corridor through the 'Look East' policy and now the 'Act East' policy of India. There is an increasing trend of financing development projects by multinational companies and banks like the Asian Development Bank, International Monetary Fund, World Bank, International Development Bank, etc. in various projects. Development projects and programmes are supposed to bring provisions for better lifestyles and benefits of society. Road expansion, transnational highway developments, mega-dam construction, oil and other natural resources exploration are the new emerging important issues which displace many indigenous people from their own villages. It aggravates people to indulge in various unwanted activities and migrate as their livelihood has been taken away in the name of development.

Displacement and marginalisation of indigenous people is not a new phenomenon. But in the case of Manipur, the Loktak Multipurpose Hydroelectric Project and Khuga dam have caused displacement of indigenous communities from their land and dispossessed them of their source of livelihood. Today, the Trans-Asian Highway construction and the controversial Mapithel dam project unleashing displacement of various communities. These projects have been introduced for promoting development and to alleviate poverty in Manipur. However, in reality, it only implies suffering for the people and forces them to migrate for their livelihood. During the interview, Thangkhal, age 27, who just completed his post-graduation from one of the reputed universities in Delhi, does not want to go back as his family land has been submerged by the Khuga dam. Most of the families have been displaced due to the construction of the dam. Most of his family members have migrated in the city including his parents and opened a grocery store in Munirka for sustenance since they have lost their paddy fields which used to be their source of livelihood.

A group of females age ranging from 18-30 years old narrated their stories of how they have migrated to Delhi after the submergence of their villages and paddy fields from the controversial Mapithel dam. All these females belong to the Tangkhul Naga community from Ukhrul district. Chadong, a small village, which used to be a famous for its fertile soil, and considered among the Tangkhuls as the rice bowl, the entire village used to depend on agricultural activities including children in collecting roots, berries, snails, oysters and fish from the rivers but the entire village has been submerged by the water and the people have been displaced. Apart from Chadong there are other villages like Phayang, Louphong, Lamlai Khullen, Lamlai Khunou, Lamlai Mongbung, Riha and Thawai which have been affected massively. Most of their rice cultivation has gone underwater. These women have left no choice but to look for another alternative source for their survival and that's how they have ended migrating to Delhi. Apni (name changed), age 28, the female, is from Riha village of Ukhrul district, currently working in one of the BPOs and taking care of her younger sibling's education in the city. Earlier their parents used to send enough money for their education but after the submergence of the rice fields their life has become hand to mouth as their source of living has been cut-off completely due to the construction of the Mapithel dam. So is the case of Chon Horam, who is working at one of the Korean restaurants as a waitress, she is just XII standard and a 25-year-old female from Chadong village which has been completely submerged by the newly constructing dam. When she was in the village her family used to depend on agricultural activities, collecting herbs and mushroom from the jungle and sell it in the nearby market called Yaingangpokpi. Earning Rs. 3,000 to 5,000 in a day was easy for them before the submergence of their village as it used to be one of the fertile land and easy to collect vegetables from the nearby hills but everything turned upside down once the entire village had gone under water and the villagers had to leave and climb up to the hill slopes and build houses temporarily. Such cases led these women group to migrate to the city like Delhi. Even after experiencing discrimination in the city yet they do not want to leave as there is no other option left for them to provide a good opportunity at their hometown or villages. Thus, in the recent within four or five year's mass migration including parents from Manipur have increased in Delhi.

Migration already disturbs the fabric and functioning of society itself in conflict-torn areas and inflicted multifaceted impacts. Women and children economically marginalised by displacement and disadvantaged by migration of their key family members are compelled to take up available jobs, detrimental to their health, rights, and security and thus exposed to a range of abuse and exploitation (Yumnam, 2018). The increasing impoverishment and migration in various part of Manipur is already a direct fall-out of the failure of the government and the project authorities to establish any concrete mechanisms to respond to the multifaceted emerging due to the implementation of huge projects. The future of these communities has been curtailed, with no provision for their education and survival means which directly or indirectly enforced them to migrate in big cities.

Another important factor which needs to be addressed here is the communal conflicts among different heterogeneous communities and insurgencies, which have destroyed hundreds of villages, thousands of lives, made many homeless or orphans and internally displaced which compel them to migrate. Three major ethnic communal conflicts occurred in Manipur were between Naga-Kuki in 1992-1999, Meitei-Pangal (Manipuri Muslim) conflict in 1993 and also Kuki-Paite conflicts in 1997-1998 (Tarapot 2005). Time to time there is a communal tension being created between the Nagas and Meiteis on the issue of integration of Naga areas. Thus, rampant attacks on the villages and villagers continued unabated and bandhs, boycotts, indefinite curfews, strikes, procession and a war of words in the newspapers, etc., have been on the rise till today which led people to migrate in neighbouring states and big cities in search of livelihood and it has become a major factor for youth seeking to migrate from Manipur.

Youth migrants from the region, particularly from Manipur, are mostly engaged in the modest profiled jobs such as in the retail shops, hotels, beauty parlours, private hospitals and clinics, call centres where job security and career advancement is a major constraint. Several youth have prolonged their stay in Delhi despite completing their studies, with financial support from their parents, sibling or even self-finance themselves by doing part-time jobs (like call centres) and strive to get better employment.

However, my recent field study conducted within South Delhi circle shows an increasing number of female migrants of age 19-32 from Ukhrul, Chandel, Tamenglong and Churachandpur districts of Manipur belonging to the Naga and Kuki communities mostly engaged in beauty parlours, restaurants and retail shops as their qualifications are just Class X-XII passed. Most of them have come from those areas which have been displaced either with communal violence or state-led development-induced displacement forced them to migrate. As per their version, most of their land has been taken away or submerged by the water bodies. There is no means of livelihood as most of them depend on agricultural activities. Some of them migrated with their families and opened groceries like selling bamboo shoots, dry fermented fish, vegetables etc. from home, meat shops and second-hand clothes shops. They feel more secure than before as they find avenues for sustenance in the capital city and wish to remain in the city only.

Delhi a Second Home (pull factor)

Delhi as the capital of India has offered numerous opportunities apart from other metropolitan cities. One can say that Delhi is not just another metropolitan city but a capital city of India. Delhi does not only welcome people across the country but also accommodates refugees from neighbouring countries like Myanmar, Bangladesh and Tibet. Delhi offers numbers of India's finest educational institutions starting from school to colleges and universities. Schools in Delhi attract a good number of children from the region where financially strong families send their children for high school education in Delhi and so for children of those parents are living in Delhi and NCR. Delhi has the finest colleges, universities and technical institutions which have also provided the best infrastructures and environment for educational opportunities with multiple choices of courses have attracted the younger generation from the region.

The city also offers the country's finest government and private hospitals where many of the youngsters can seek professional jobs and many people come for their treatments. With the advent of globalisation and economic liberalisation, the capital city does offer multiple avenues for people who come to seek opportunities not necessarily for government jobs but in various private sectors. There are numbers of private and multinational companies where people can easily find jobs even with a modest qualification. Comparatively Northeast people being more literate than the other parts of India has shown various job prospects in private companies in Delhi. The better amenities and facilities provided in the capital city wooed numbers of youth of the region.

When we look at the literacy rate as per the data published by the 2011 Census, we can clearly see the picture of the high literacy rate among the Northeast states. India has managed to achieve an effective literacy rate of 74.04 per cent in 2011. However, the literacy rate of the Northeast states is always high comparatively with other states.

Now many young people of the region in Delhi can support themselves while continuing their studies, or support their family members to study. The young Northeast migrants, in general, have begun to create a niche in certain labour markets, and also the labour recruiters are travelling to the important cities of the region to offer jobs in call centres, restaurants, hotels and spas. As getting through in central government jobs is relatively easy because many of them belong to the Scheduled Tribes and Scheduled Castes[2] category. Moreover, there are:

1. No specific mother tongue education among the tribal communities, rather they have been trained in English medium.
2. Command over the English language among the youth from the region gets more opportunities for various job offers in Delhi etc.

The opening up of new employment opportunities in the cities particularly in metropolitan cities like Delhi acted as the pull factor for migration. The concentration of the availability of job in big cities helps to benefit mostly the educated youth and those who can afford to reach the destination. In recent years, it is clearly shown that migration is rapidly growing from the periphery as mentioned above that having command over English gets more job opportunities in Delhi. Nevertheless, in general, northeast people's nature of hospitality or the English accent helps in getting job easily in hotel/retail shops or in customer care services (*see* Marchang, 2011).

When something unwanted happens to them, it does not take much time to react as the majority of people from the region stays in group in certain pockets of the city. In fact, Nido Tania, a student from Arunachal Pradesh had an altercation with some locals at Lajpat Nagar. Tania succumbed the next day which provoked the entire northeast people who stay in the city. After much of public outcry in city for proper justification, restructuring policy implementation, the Bezbaruah Committee[3] was constituted and civil society bodies take up the initiatives of helping and reaching out to the northeast people in their dire situation. Their rigorous demands and the large section from academics, institutions continuous debates and discourses on the series of targeting northeast youth left no choice for the government but to instruct Delhi Police to take up stringent steps and punish the perpetrators. Among the colleges and universities, they have appointed the Dean of Northeast students to provide support when any form of difficulties comes to the students. In between, the Delhi Police also started taking up various safety measures, awareness programmes and media sensitisation. Even after so many unfortunate incidents, the recent step taken up by the Delhi Police are gradually appreciating by the Northeast migrant yet racial discrimination against them remains the same. Even though, each year the number of youth migration keeps increasing to expand their horizon.

Visibility of Northeast Youth in the Public Sphere

Majority of people from mainland India assume that people of the region have come under Scheduled Tribe category only and reservation has helped them come out into the mainstream because they have been consistently side-lined. As most of the mainland people have less knowledge about the region, geographically, physically and culturally. There is a gap between the Northeast and the rest of India. Some feel that reservation helps them come out and be a part of the mainstream through this people gets to engage with the Northeast people. In most of the metropolitan cities including the capital city, there is a stereotypical mindset that people who migrate from the region belong to reservation categories which is not entirely correct. Some of them do belong to reservation categories but not everybody in the region[4], however, one should also not undermine the existence of certain groups who are in the general category. Reserved category people from another part of India who have come to the capital city or in other metropolitan cities availed the same reservation facilities just like the youth of this region, however, they do not face any kind of challenges meted by the Northeast people. One can understand that it is not just about a matter of availing reservation but because of their physical appearance, cultural differences which are easily distinguishable from the other.[5]

Young northeast migrants are highly visible (and audible) in certain service jobs. In call centres, workers are trained to 'neutralise their accents, and call monitoring, scripting', and 'locational masking' are all crucial components of call centre work. This has advantages for young Northeast migrants (Duncan, 2012). I would also agree with Duncan, as per my own fieldwork—most of the Manipuri youth who are working in the call centres, hotels, retail shops are mainly from the hilly areas, however, have attended English medium schools. There are other factors affecting language in different parts of the region: for instance, insurgents have banned screening of Hindi films in Manipur. As a result, most youths do not have typically Indian-accented English which always stands out. Youth migrants of the region, in general, are unmarried and in their 20s to early 30s, most of them do not have children or have left their children with relatives back home. This makes them able to work in shifts in various private sectors. As such they have become desirable as a 'flexible' and well-qualified workforce for the burgeoning call centre industry. In retail, they find work in clothing stores, sports stores, spas and cosmetic stores. Men are especially well represented in stores and restaurants that project a global brand image, while women, sometimes, are cast in sexualised roles, particularly in fashion stores, restaurants and spas.

Challenges Faced by Manipuri Youth in Delhi

Outside the enclosed spaces of malls and call centres, youth migrants face a number of challenges in their everyday lives. For many migrants in general, racism characterises their experience of Delhi. There is a negative perception towards people of the region. They consider these young men and women, especially the women, as of loose character and label them even as prostitute. In general, they have different notion of projecting them and passing comments as *chinki*, *momo*, *bahadur* and other derogatory remarks. There are various instances where the house owners, landlords and caretakers abused based on racial discrimination. The face of northeast youth in general, and Manipuri youth in particular, have clear distinctive features from the others. Northeast people are generally projected as outsiders/ foreigners because of their physical affinity with the other South Asian or East Asian people and the gaps between culture, language, lifestyle, physical appearance, food habits etc. and thus not acceptable easily as Indians.

Finding accommodation is another big challenge for every migrant who have come to the capital city or in any other part of the metropolitan city unless they are very rich or whose relatives or friends are already in the city. Generally, people end up living in either rented house or the flats except some of the students who are lucky to avail hostel facilities in their respective universities or colleges. Majority of the youth who work in the BPO sectors, retail shops and hospitality sectors like beauty parlours, spas and hotels are mostly relying on the rented houses or the flats. In various instances the landlord over charge more than the actual amount as there is not fixed amount as such, sometimes the landlord even evicted whenever they wanted and even use their muscle powers to exercise their superiority. There are also various instances where the landlords, shopkeepers, auto drivers put false allegations on the youth of the region which led to major altercations and many times ended up losing their precious lives like Nido Tania's case. In my field work, some students from Manipur who stay in the rented house in Kotla Mubarakpur told that they pay taxes for the way they look and different features from the mainland. Not just the difference of physical appearance but there is a language barrier as they have their own native languages and English is their second language that is the reason why they hardly speak Hindi; that is the reason why the brokers and property dealers take full advantage of the weakness in language.

Another challenge for female migrant is to face sexual abuse — physically and mentally; projected as of loose character and prostitutes; looks down in public places. In the centre or another part of India woman are subdued in terms of their visibility in public sphere which is not in the case of Northeast, women's participation in the public sphere are very open as much as men do. No men in the Northeast will ever think because women come out of the home and participate in public life to be easy prey for sexual assault. But in Delhi, it is the opposite and they consider migrant females from the Northeast are of loose character as they are free and mix with their counterparts.

Due to socio-political unrest, mainly Manipuri youth migrate to Delhi in the hope of a better standard of life and job opportunities. But in the course of it, they face a number of challenges. They are socially discriminated and sexually violated. When they face racial attack and sexual violence, their educational careers, jobs, and business also get affected massively (Duncan, 2012). Facing racial discrimination has become a part of daily life for a majority of youth coming from the Northeast to the national capital, which touts its tag of being a cosmopolitan city. Women from the region undergo traumatic experiences daily while living in the national capital region including molestation, eve teasing, sexual harassment, etc. Whether public transport, educational institutions or workplace, Manipuri youth feel those belonging to so-called mainland India discriminate them due to their different facial features, hairstyle, dressing sense, food habits and language. Despite hailing from the geopolitical space of India, they face racial abuse yet they are forced to overlook these instances for the sake of survival.

Cultural gap, food habit difference, physical appearance difference, less support system, eve teasing, sexual abuse, physical abuse, passing lewd comments, projected as very exotic, taking advantage for being over-friendly especially in the public places, workplaces and rented accommodation, etc., are common indicators. When they face racial attack and sexual violence, their educational careers, jobs and business get affected. Yet, they prefer to stay in the city. The challenges faced by them have a paradigm shift from racial attack to sexual violence and sexual violence to human trafficking, as it is turning into a severe form of challenges for the youth migrants, especially among the women.

Racial Attack: Racial attack against Northeast people in big cities has become so common especially in Delhi. The local people always differentiate Northeast people by their unique features and appearance, and abuse them with derogatory terms. When they resist against these abusers, they become victim and end up suffering physically, verbally and mentally.

Sexual Violence: Rape and murder of eight years old girl at Mahipalpur in Delhi on April 2009. After she was raped and murdered, the accused dumped her inside the neighbour's water tank.

The gangrape of a 20-year-old Delhi University student at Dhaula Kuan in a moving car took place in May 2005. She was abducted while walking back home after buying food from a roadside eatery. One of the accused, who was caught, was sentenced to 14 years' imprisonment by a court while the remaining three accused are still absconding.

There was rape of a 30-yearold BPO employee in November 2010. Five men, intoxicated with liquor, raped the woman for over 40 minutes in a moving vehicle. She was forced into the vehicle near Nanakpura Gurdwara and was later found in a semi-conscious state in Mangolpuri Industrial Estate. It took more than one hour for the police to find her after she dialled '100' and informed the police. These are some of the accounts which have been collected from the newspapers and Internet.

Human Trafficking: As per the numerous local media reports from the past many years, a number of young girls are found missing and kidnapped every day but no progress of their rescue is made known to the general public through any media. There should be regular reporting of progress by the Delhi Police who are searching for the missing persons.

In early 2015, a small survey was conducted among the Manipuri youth residing in South Delhi, places like Munirka, Safdurjung, Mohamadpur, Kishangarh, Humayunpur, Kotla Mubarakpur, Ashram, Moti Bagh, South

Extension, Chirag Delhi and Mahipalpur. Respondent including both male and female of the average age of 18 years to 35 years of age were the target group. Most of them work in the private companies including call centres, hotels, beauty parlours and spas, some in the aviation sector as fly stewards, private banks and some of them have even opened second-hand clothes store. Their qualifications are mostly X and XII pass and some of them are pursuing graduation through distance course mode while they are also working. When enquired about their stay in the city, most of the respondent were not very happy, rather disappointed with the treatment or hindrances they meet in their daily lives while commuting in local transportation, getting lewd comments, mental harassment given by their rent owners, etc.

There is always a concern about their safety as the crime against women keep increasing in the city and targeting Northeast people never stopped even after the implementation of North East Cell in the city. They cannot stay freely as there are constant restrictions in the food habits, movements, gathering with friends and relatives, continuous increasing of the rent amount as it has become an ongoing process even after so much of efforts, it keeps on putting from various sections.

Government and Civil Society Response

Nido Tania's death had drawn large attention from every section of the society. In 2016 the Supreme Court asked the central government to set up a suitable mechanism or nodal agency to oversee and pursue implementation of the recommendations made by the Bezbaruah Committee. Not only in relation to the prevention of crime against people from the region but also in relation to creating a conducive atmosphere for such communities from the far east to get proper assimilation in the mainstream society. The court had also taken note of the recommendation by the said committee which has suggested amendment of Section 153 IPC to make racial slur a distinct offence. A number of steps have been taken for sensitisation of local police on the issue of discrimination against Northeast people. An officer of the rank of joint commissioner of police has been appointed as the nodal officer for northeast migrant issues.

Academic and policy-research institutions need to produce print and digital media and scholarly works to reach out as large an audience as possible, through their research works to be available and share with policy-makers and lawmakers, as guidance for youth as they feel left out somewhere or the other from the main domain. The benefits of developmental policies have not reached equitably. Every tribe in the region has its own way of life and people have to accept these differences. The political leaders of the region have come forward to address the problems faced by their communities in the national capital.

The sensitising needs to be carried out at various levels and platforms. To tackle and attempt preventing the issue, more sensitisation seminars are required, in which the safety measurement on the parts of northeast communities can be uttered in practical ways. Cultural integration by adopting local churches, different student bodies can be a crucial part from northeast migrant in the national capital. Media has done well in taking up their plight and their contributions require to take more interest and initiative in bringing the issue to the national limelight and taking an important role in bridging the gap between Northeast and the rest of the country.

Conclusion

Migration to the big cities has become a trend in the present scenario, a trend of push factors for youth from the periphery. Push factors like low income, dependence on agriculture, lack of proper educational infrastructure, search for a better lifestyle, unemployment, ethnic violence, arms conflict, an increasing rate of displacement, land encroachment by the government in the name of development are crucial examples associated with the place of origin. Lack of educational infrastructure with a limited choice of studies is most affected by the socio-political crisis in the northeast. Serious steps taken to invest and develop educational infrastructure with more professional studies will help in reducing youth migration. To tackle the shortage of employment opportunity in finding suitable government jobs, the absence of public and private industries, the rapid decline in agricultural activities in the home state. If the state government gives full attention and opens various avenues for people returning to home states after gaining professional academic and skill training, it will help in bringing development project in the state.

The main pull factor leading to migration is due to the enormous availability of educational infrastructures with multiple choices, followed by mushrooming multinational companies of employment opportunities in the capital city of Delhi and high demand for English speaking youth. It is understandable that despite a high literacy rate, the region is characterised by a visible lack of adequate avenues for higher or technical education or vocational training as they have limited infrastructure. Another issue with respect to employment is the nature of work many people have been engaging, undermining the kind of discrimination they have met in their day to day lives in the cities.

This is the high time one must acknowledge the credibility and potentials of northeast youth. Instead of having a stereotypical mindset towards them rather they should see their potential and contribute to the country. There will always be difference between people coming from Northeast India to people who stay in North India or South India, and this is the beauty of having unity and diversity of India. Acceptance and anticipation are the new words one must accommodate when it comes to bridge the gap between one region to another region and learn from one another which they do not have.

The racial discrimination and sexual violence faced by Northeast men and women have been highlighted for quite a long time, yet no positive sign of political will is shown so far. Until and unless the political-will fully comes forward, the struggle to prevent and reduce racial discrimination and sexual violence will remain unresolved although within the last two or three years we can see some improvement.

It is a mistake of the policy-makers (educationalists) for not including them since the past 70 years for not understanding the importance and for not including in the (school) books, all the information and the knowledge of the Northeast. This is a drawback in our educational system and the sooner they correct it, the better it will be. Not because Delhi and North India become a safer place for the Northeast people, but it is because the Northeast is very much part of India as much as an Indian in this country. It is very important that consciousness is made to rise in these kinds of situation.

Notes

1. The field work was conducted in the beginning of the year 2015 as part of my studies in some selected places where the Manipuri people resides in the city.
2. Only about 27 per cent of the Northeast population are Scheduled Tribes but in Delhi or elsewhere, the Northeast region is seen as a tribal land.
3. The Bezbaruah Committee, headed by M.P Beazbaruah, was constituted in 2014 after the death of Nido Tania. The Committee's mandate was to listen and look into the various issues raised by people from the Northeast living in other areas of the country, especially in the metro cities.
4. One must not forget that in the entire Northeast region there were four independent kingdoms before they became part of India.
5. People who migrate from the other part of the country specially the Northern, Western and the Southern parts of India.

References

Davis, Kingsley. 1961. 'Urbanisation in India: Past and Future', in Roy Turner (ed.) *India's Urban Future*. Berkeley: University of California Press, 3-26.

Duncan, McDuie-Ra, (ed.). 2012. *Northeast migrants in Delhi: Race, Refuge and Retail*. Amsterdam: Amsterdam University Press.

Duncan, McDuie-Ra. 2012a). 'Cosmopolitan tribals: frontier migrants in Delhi', *South Asia Research* 32/1, 39-55.

Duncan, McDuie-Ra. 2013. 'Beyond the 'exclusionary city': North-East migrants in neoliberal Delhi', *Urban Studies* 50(8), 1625-1640.

Duncan, McDuie-Ra. 2015. 'Is India Racist?: Murder, Migration and Mary Kom', *South Asia: Journal of South Asian Studies* 38(2), 304–319.

Duncan, McDuie-Ra. 2016. 'Adjacent identities in Northeast India', *Journal Asian Ethnicity* 17(3).

Eastern Quarterly. 2013. *AFSPA and the Spaces of Women* 9(III & IV) Autumn & Winter.

Government of Delhi. 2018. *Economic Survey Delhi Report* (2017-2018). New Delhi.

Government of India. 2005. Report of the Committee to Review the Armed Forces (Special Powers) Acts, 1958. New Delhi: Ministry of Home Affairs.

Kundu, Amitabh. 2007. 'Mobility of Population', in Kaushik Basu (ed), *The Oxford Companion to Economics in India*. New Delhi: Oxford University Press.

North East Support Centre & Helpline. 2011. North East Migration and Challenges in National Capital Cities: An Abstract of Research Project Report. New Delhi: North East Support Centre & Helpline.

Oinam, Bhagat. 2003. 'Patterns of Ethnic Conflict in the North-East: A Study on Manipur', *Economic and Political Weekly*, 38(21), 2031-2037.

Ramesh Babu, P. 2012. *Migration from North-East to Urban Centres: A Study of Delhi Region*, NLI Research Studies Series, No. 094/2012. Noida: V.V. Giri National Labour Institute.

Reimeingam, Marchang. 2011. 'Unemployment, Job Aspiration and Migration: A Case Study of Tangkhul Migrants to Delhi', *Eastern Quarterly*, 7(3&4).

Srivastava, R. And Sasikumar, S.K. 2003. 'A Review of Migration in India, Its Impact and Key Issues', Paper Presented at the Regional Conference on Migration, Development and Pro-Poor Policy Choices in Asia, held in Dhaka from 22 to 24th June.

Tarapot, Phanjoubam. 2005. *Bleeding Manipur*. New Delhi: Har-Anand Publications.

Usha Devi, M.D. and U.A. Shimray. 2010. Report on Migration from the North Eastern Region: A Study of Educated Youth from NER in Bangalore and Delhi. Bangalore: ISEC.

Weissbrodt, David and Rumsey, Mary (ed.). 2011. *Vulnerable and Marginalised Groups and Human Rights*. Edward Elgar Publishing Limited, UK.

Yumnam, Jiten. 2018. 'Unfolding Mapithel Dam Implications & State Unaccountability', *Imphal Free Press*, 7 April.

9

Rethinking Higher Education in Northeast India

Sangeeta Angom and *M. Stelin Singh*

Educational development in Northeast India has historically been not so encouraging. The requirement in the education sector of the region is also different from other parts of the country. Thus, while today the region has high literacy rate, but the quality of education is a concern.

Historically, the development of education in Northeast India is not so encouraging in comparison with the rest of the country. The region is different in many ways from other regions as far as the needs and priorities in the education sector are concerned. The North Eastern Regional Education Council (2010) has reported that the region has high literacy rate but quality as well standard of education is of a great concern. Moreover, the lack of adequate educational infrastructure in the region compells large numbers of students to go to other parts of the country for their higher studies.

The current scenario of higher education in the region in terms of access, size, enrolment, the number of teachers and the teacher-pupil ratio is briefly discussed (*see* All India Survey on Higher Education, 2016–17). Higher education in India is characterised by extreme regional disparities in access, participation and expenditure. The access to higher education assessed in terms of availability of colleges per lakh population in the age group of 18–23 revealed that in 2012–13, altogether 15 states and union territories have greater access to higher education as compared to the national average of 28 institutions per lakh population while it was nearly absent in Lakshadweep. The access in Telangana (with 59 institutions) has the highest and Bihar has the lowest with only seven institutions.

Manipur scored the eleventh rank among top 15 states in terms of access to higher education. The state has better access to college in the region as compared to the national average. The average enrolment per college in most of the states of the region, such as Manipur, Arunachal Pradesh, Tripura, Meghalaya and Assam are higher than all India average (659). The Northeast region has 54 university/university level institutions which is 7.1% of all India. In this region, Assam has the highest number (18) followed by Meghalaya (9), Arunachal Pradesh (8), Sikkim (6), Manipur (4), Mizoram (2), Nagaland (4) and Tripura (3). There are several private universities too. There are altogether 798 colleges (2.2% of India) out of which 24 per cent colleges are private-aided/unaided. Sikkim (17) and Arunachal Pradesh (20) have the lowest number of colleges in the region while Assam (491) has the largest number of colleges, followed by Manipur (75), Nagaland (64), Tripura (51), Meghalaya (50) and Mizoram (30).

The region lacks specialised higher education institutions like medical, agriculture and law. Majority of the universities and colleges of the region are of traditional general education. There are only 14 technical universities—Assam (4), Manipur (2), Meghalaya (2) and Mizoram (2), Arunachal Pradesh (1), Sikkim (1), Nagaland (1) and Tripura (1). Except for Assam and Manipur, there is no agricultural university in other states although agriculture is the main occupation of the people. Further, there are no medical colleges/universities in several states of the region. There is a need to establish more specialised institutions. Similarly, the region lacks colleges which offer specialised courses. Colleges offering courses in medical, management, veterinary, and pharmacy are unevenly distributed among the states.

The share of northeastern states to the national average is only three per cent of total enrolment in higher education at all levels and also the enrolment of women is 3.1 per cent of the total enrolment. The region has an equal share of enrolment of both male and female population. Assam, the most populous state of the region, has the highest enrolment (77%) while Sikkim has the lowest enrolment (3.5%). Manipur recorded 12 per cent enrolment at higher education at various levels followed by Meghalaya (10%), Tripura (10%), Arunachal Pradesh (6%), Nagaland (5%) and Mizoram (4%). In terms of women enrolment, except for Tripura, other states of the region have higher enrolment of women in institutions of higher education.

There is higher proportion of students enrolled in Arts courses constituting about 97.3 lakh out of which 47.1 per cent are males and 52.9 per cent are females. Science is the second major stream with 47.3 lakh in which male students constitute 52.4 per cent and female students constitute 47.6 per cent. Engineering and technology is the third major stream with 41.6 lakh students enrolled. The enrolment in several branches of engineering: mechanical (9.5 lakh), computer (8.0 lakh), electronics (6.9 lakh), civil (6.3 lakh) and electrical (4.4 lakh). The number of students enrolled in the commerce stream is 40.0 lakh in which 52.5 per cent are male students and 47.5 per cent are female students. In the information technology/computer application stream, there are 6.9 lakh students enrolled. Medical science stream shows a different picture with high enrolment of about 6.0 lakh female students out of 9.8 lakh total enrolment. In the management courses, there are 5.6 lakh students with about 3.4 lakh male students. The students enrolled in law courses are 3.5 lakh out of which 2.4 lakh are males.

The gross enrolment ratio (GER) in higher education in the region is less than the all India level; however, for the Scheduled Castes and the Scheduled Tribes, it is higher than the all India level. Sikkim has the highest GER for all categories with 37.3 per cent followed by Manipur (35.0%) and Arunachal Pradesh (31.2%). The GER in Assam is far below with 17.2 per cent only. The GER for the Scheduled Castes is the highest in Mizoram (108.9%), followed by Manipur (57.5%), Meghalaya (48.1%), Sikkim (26.3%), Assam (19.0%) and Tripura (17.9%). The GER for the Scheduled Tribes is the highest in Arunachal Pradesh with 31.2 per cent followed by Sikkim (27.1%), Mizoram (24.3%), Assam (22.5%), Manipur (20.2%), Meghalaya (19.3%), Nagaland (16.0%) and Tripura (13.7%).

There are 37,376 teachers in higher education institutions across the region in which 58 per cent are male teachers. Among the Scheduled Tribes category, the share of female teacher accounts to 53 per cent of the total. Assam has the highest number of teachers (57%), while Arunachal Pradesh has the lowest number of teachers (3%). Mizoram reported having the highest number of temporary teachers constituting about nine per cent of the total teachers in the state. Arunachal Pradesh has the lowest number of temporary teachers constituting about 1.4 per cent of the total teachers in the state.

Out-migrants from Northeast India

Every year, a large number of students have been going out to major cities of the country for their studies. The region which comprises about 3.7 per cent of the total population of the country has 2.1 per cent share of in-migrants and 2.7 per cent out-migrants respectively. The states of the region having higher out-migrants than in-migrants are Mizoram (5%), Nagaland (4.3%), Manipur (1.7%) and Assam (1.3%). Based on the NSS 64th Report, the trend of out-migrants from the region has been worked out and discussed below.

Rural male migrants accounted for about 76 per cent of the total out-migrants who have migrated for employment purposes. The main reason for female out-migrants from the rural areas has predominantly been due to their marriage, which accounted for nearly 57 per cent of female out-migrants from rural areas. It is also found that a significantly higher proportion of females (21%) from the rural areas have migrated for their studies compared to the male out-migrants (19%). While the majority of the male out-migrants (69%) from the urban areas have been due to employment but for the female out-migrants from urban areas, the marriage has been the main reason for migration (48%). It is found that a significantly higher proportion of females from the urban areas (24%) have migrated for their studies compared to the male out-migrants (22%).

Majority of the male migrants from both the rural (76%) and the urban (69%) areas have migrated for employment-related reasons. For female migrants from both the rural (55%) and urban (55%) areas, the reasons for out-migration have been predominantly due to marriage. It is also found that a significantly higher proportion of females from both the rural and urban areas have migrated for their studies. For the purpose of their studies, nearly 21 per cent females have migrated from rural areas and 24 per cent from urban areas while the corresponding share for males was 19 per cent and 22 per cent in rural and urban areas respectively.

For the purpose of studies, except for Manipur and Meghalaya, in other states, the male migrants outnumbered female migrants both from rural and urban areas. Manipur recorded 38 per cent female migrant from urban areas while Meghalaya recorded 30 per cent female migrants from urban areas. Whereas the corresponding shares of males from both the states were 10 per cent and 20 per cent respectively. Sikkim has the highest share of male migrants for the purpose of studies with 54 per cent from urban areas. Assam has the least number of male migrants at eight per cent from the urban areas. Meghalaya has a maximum number of migrants from rural areas (42%) whereas Assam has the least migrants from rural areas (0.9%). The migrants for the purpose of studies are more from the urban areas than the rural areas of the region. It is found that a significantly higher proportion of females from both the rural and urban areas have migrated for their studies. The female migrants from both urban and rural areas of the region are significantly predominant, at nearly 22 per cent of female migrants.

One of the issues relating to the migration of students from the region is the decline of students from the sending state(s). This can have a rather detrimental impact on the economy by depleting the already scarce resources. Further, there are also worries about brain drain as a large number of people with technical skills have migrated. It is generally agreed that students from the region came to Delhi, Bengaluru, Pune, Chennai and other places to pursue their studies. The main push factors responsible for out-migrants of students relating to study are:

(1) *Lack of institutions with quality infrastructure*: Lack of institutions with quality infrastructure and a limited choice of courses in most of higher education institutions of the region are the main factor which pushes the students to go out for higher studies. As on 2017-18, there were only 826 colleges, 89 universities and 11 institutes of national importance in the region. Majority of the universities offer traditional general education with very few technical universities. Only three states have agricultural universities. Except for Assam, there are no medical and law universities in the region. Similarly, there are limited numbers of specialised colleges. Majority of them offer traditional general education. Teacher education is fairly distributed among the states. Specialised institutions of medical, management, veterinary, pharmacy, etc. are unevenly distributed among the states of the region. Moreover, the government schools have poor infrastructure. The parents who are financially better off manage to send their children for better education to different cities of the country.

(2) *Lack of educational opportunities*: There is a disparity between demand for and supply of technical and professional education. There are a lesser number of professional institutions except in Assam. We see that migrants from Assam are the least in comparison with states like Manipur, Tripura and Meghalaya.

(3) *Lack of employment opportunities*: As per NSS 64th round, the majority of the out-migrants from the region are for employment purposes. This shows that the region lacks job opportunities. There is a lack of entrepreneurship and industries where educated people can be employed. Moreover, corruption in the recruitment of government jobs has been disturbing. Only those who have money and political connection can get government job. It is also rightly pointed out that private sector companies do not invest in the region due to the socio-political crisis.

(4) *Socio-political unrest*: Socio-political unrest in states like Manipur has also affected development activities. Constant public strikes, bandhs, curfew are some of the major features of socio-political unrest in the region. For example, there was a strike against the demand for removal of the Vice Chancellor of Manipur University. This has affected the academic life of the students. The university was shut down for several months. Frequent strikes affected the livelihood of the people and the overall economic development. The young generations of the region especially from those affected states were compelled to migrate elsewhere for studies and employment.

(5) *Communal conflict*: Apart from numerous insurgencies, the region has witnessed a number of violent conflicts involving different communities. These violent conflicts have displaced many people from their homes. Among them, many children who are internally displaced are not able to return to their schools. Thus, violence has become a factor for young people seeking to migrate from the region.

Besides, there are several pull factors, such as better education and better employment opportunities in prosperous parts of the country.

Challenges of Higher Education

Besides, the above-mentioned factors in particular for out-migration for studies, there are other challenges in the higher education sector. Higher education in the region is characterised as 'single track' education system with a generic curriculum and within that major concentration is Arts streams. Curriculum in the universities and colleges is still found to be rigid, bookish, and it is irrelevant to the real problem of the society. The outdated curriculum is not suitable for changing needs of the society. The universities in the region, as a result, have been producing unfit, unemployed and unemployable graduates. However, some parts of the region are still experiencing conflict where the militant activities are halting development process. The curriculum revisions for employability should assume special importance in these states. Higher education should have a special social responsibility in curbing insurgency problem, generate employment opportunities and create values of coexistence. Development of human resource also acquires importance in the region in view of the Act East policy. It is expected that there will be an international trade and commerce flowing through the region.

There has been the limited experience of curriculum innovation based on the initiative of some of the colleges. However, curriculum revision and the introduction of new programmes have suffered due to lack of government support. Besides, the teaching-learning processes in most of the institutions are one way and integration of technology is still poor in most of the institutions especially in colleges. The learner-centered approach, in particular, has added a new dimension and paradigm shift to the teaching-learning process. Teachers in the region for a variety of reasons follow the traditional practice of lecture method and have not changed their practices. The learner-centered approach under the semester system requires knowledge, freedom and environment to follow the innovative practices.

It is also true that various academic reform programmes are being initiated in the region. But, these academic reform programmes will make sense only when the effective teaching-learning process is made operational at the institutional level and teachers are motivated to follow innovative practices in the teaching-learning process.

It has been also learnt that most of the colleges in the region have shortage of teachers and as a result of increasing number of students every year, the teacher-student ratio in colleges of almost all the states of the region has become much higher than the specified ratio of 1:20 by the University Grants Commission (UGC). As a result of this, not only teachers are over-burdened, but several colleges in this region are not being able to initiate the process of NAAC accreditation. Further, the accreditation has become mandatory for obtaining permanent affiliation from respective universities. As such, most of the colleges have found themselves in a difficult position of not being able to apply either for NAAC accreditation or for permanent affiliation and, therefore, most of them are not able to apply for various funding schemes given by UGC for the development of colleges.

The other important challenges are that the education system is still examination oriented and many of the government institutions lack student-friendly infrastructure. Trained and motivated teachers are also lacking in many of the higher education institutions. There is also the issue of underpaid teachers, for instance, in many cases, the part-time teachers, especially in the states of Meghalaya and Manipur, are underpaid. Further, one could feel the need to improve the working condition and culture of work in the institutions. Funding is also another challenge as the majority of the government aided colleges are suffering from proper funding. Thus, there are numerous challenges in higher education institutions in the region.

Lessons Learned and the Way Forward

Thinking on the line with the Act East Policy and for improving the economic condition of the region, development of the higher education sector in the region is so important. There is also a need to make the region as an education hub to attract students not only from other parts of the country but also from the neighbouring countries. Moreover, reducing the number of out-migrants for study and also for job opportunities should be an important agenda of the government. For that, first of all, one needs to address those issues which are related to the slow growth of higher education in the region. In this context, based on the above discussions, some of the suggestions or strategies to be adopted are listed below. There is a need to upgrade the existing higher education institutions especially the state universities and government colleges in terms of providing better infrastructure. Governance-related issues related to universities need to be addressed and settled down quickly. There is also a need to train non-teaching staffs with new technologies. Merit-based student financing should be introduced and should ensure admissions to meritorious students independent of financial background. Internationalisation of education is the need of the hour for the region. This would entail aligning different aspects of education (curriculum, faculty, etc.) to international standards. There is a need for creating an enabling research environment in most of the universities. This would involve creating adequate means of research funding and practical applications of research. Having high-quality faculty in higher education institutions is so important in the region. Therefore, the need of the hour is to create a conducive environment for higher education institutions and provide incentives to attract and retain high-quality faculty. Introduction of faculty exchange or student exchange programme at the institution level or at the state level should be another initiative. Priority should be given on curriculum revision or introduction of those courses which are in demand and employment oriented, need-based curriculum, technology-oriented curriculum which allows hands-on training and regular evaluation and frequent curriculum upgradation. The idea of mainstreaming of young people from the region into the larger national and global economy will require equipping them directly with employable skills in professions that are in demand and correspond to worldwide. So, there is a need to improve IT and ITES sectors and also engineering, nursing, hospitality, law and agriculture. People of the region have innate talent and interest in fashion technology and product design, sports and physical fitness and music, those based on indigenous materials such as bamboo, silk, traditional textiles and so on (Ministry of Development of North Eastern Region, 2008). Along with this line, the curriculum can be developed and introduced in colleges.

References

Government of India, 2017. *All India Survey on Higher Education (2016-17)*. New Delhi: Ministry of Human Resources Development.

Ministry of Development of North Eastern Region, 2008. *North East Region Vision Document, 2020*. Agartala.

National Sample Survey Office. 2012. *Employment & Unemployment and Migration Survey: NSS 64th Round: July 2007-June 2008*. New Delhi: Ministry of Statistics and Programme Implementation.

North Eastern Regional Education Council. 2010. *Revamping of Education in the Region*. Shillong: North Eastern Council.

10

Migration and Civil Society

An Assessment from Manipur

Ningthoujam Rameshchandra

Manipur, which was once a sparsely populated area, has recently witnessed a heavy influx of migrants. As a result, it has become an issue in space, settlement and resource distribution. Such a scenario of influx has attracted the attention of some civil society groups who have registered democratic protest demanding stringent migration policy in order to monitor the unregulated influx of migrants. The author analyses the pull factors of migration into Manipur using secondary information, historical antecedents and observed facts, and also tries to inquire the matters on why the Manipuri society that accommodated migrant population without much ado in the past has now appeared to be more un-accommodative towards the migrants from the mainland of the country.

Although migration is generally considered to be intimately related to economic (Ravenstein, 1985), and social development (Sjaastad, 1962) that often resulted from development imbalances (Ninna, 2003), it is still too diverse and multifaceted to be explained by a single theory (Arango, 2000). On the other hand, assessments of the influence of migration on development have also varied over time: sometimes it has been seen as beneficial and at others detrimental to development, depending on the historical moment and circumstances (Ninna, 2003). Of course, from a neo-classical standpoint, migration does influence in the socio-economic development of the receiving as well as sending countries (Sjaastad, 1962) but very recently (and particularly in the developed countries) the migrants are often seen as a threat to the national security, particularly since the post-9/11 twin tower bombing in the US (Valeriano, 2009). Albeit clear linkages between migration and national security are yet to be established, but this aspect can no longer be ignored. In fact, migration has become a standardised problem for the developed countries to deal with (Andreas, 2003). Fears of the 'other' or internal destabilisation caused by the influx of migrants has recently become a serious concern (Valeriano, 2009).

In developing countries too, we have witnessed resistance or the sense of insecurity vis-à-vis the migrant community. However, such resistance movements are not only about national security per se but it appears to be more in terms of space, settlement, resource distribution and most significantly a perceived threat to the ethnic identity of the native population. Take, for instance, the Malays of Malaysia began to use *Bhumiputra* – 'son of the soil' (Weiner, 1978) in their resistance narratives, which was mainly emanated from the threat of Chinese influx. The civil war in Nigeria during the late 1960s was also largely based on the clash between the Igbo migrants and native population. As Weiner (1978) argued that such conflict occurred because the inter-ethnic relationship in a multi-ethnic society of the developing world usually shows such hostile characters. He further argued that such a situation arises because migration can change both the demographic and economic balance of the receiving group(s) within a given space. To Weiner (1978), "the 'protection' of space and the economic opportunities that exist within are often central objectives of the local population, while the expansion of opportunities within the space is a central objective of migrants". As a result, migration within a multi-ethnic set up is often seen as detrimental to development because it often tends to arouse intense conflict.

There arises a similar situation in Manipuri society too. This society apparently accommodated migrant population without much ado in the pre-merger period[1]. But very recently they appeared to be more reactive in approach that manifests in their movements. It was since the late 1980s that some sections of the civil society groups began to register democratic movement demanding for the enactment of the inner line permit[2] (or similar measure) to monitor the influx of unregulated migrants, and this will be discussed in the following sections.

Migration into Manipur

It may be noted here that migration into Manipur albeit occurred from the very early period, the causes or the motives behind it were different from one stream to another. From the ancient time down to the modern period, the migrants entered into Manipur on three different occasions.

Firstly, in the ancient period, the migrants were brought either as war captives or came as travellers to explore the land. What is interesting here is that among other things, the importance of war captives could be viewed in two different ways. On one hand, they can be counted as one essential aspect in understanding the mode of assimilating people into the Manipuri society[3] in earlier times. On the other hand, apart from political issues, from the economic aspect their importance was significant, in the sense that they supplemented the required labour for agriculture and other manual works, and so on. During the medieval period, most migrants came as refugees, fortune seekers or as invitees by the kings for state purposes such as interpreters, writers, priests, etc. As such, till the second quarter of the 20th century, Manipur was a melting pot, but now, new forms of migration have emerged as a consequence of the search for livelihood or very recently, on account of the impact of climate change, particularly from Bangladesh. There may be other forms of migration linked to various issues, such as nationalising frontier space (Baruah, 2007), ethnic conflict or displacement due to infrastructural installations.

Before Manipur's merger with India, the erstwhile kingdom put in place a migration policy through the department called the Foreigner's Mauzadar Office that was constituted in 1903, which helped to build a common culture shared by ethnic groups and to mitigate possible ethnic tension (UCM, 2005). But this policy was abolished soon after Manipur merged with India. This resulted, among other things, in an enormous increase in the migrant population. According to the Census of India 2001, the number of migrants has exceeded that of tribal population (Table 10.1). This has alarmed the local population, which democratically registered the protest by demanding the enactment of inner line permit or similar legislation to monitor the unregulated influx of migrants. Further, the influx also alarmed the armed opposition groups.[4] Of course, Manipur has not experienced violent clashes between the migrants and native population as

Table 10.1: Estimated Population Composition of Manipur for the year 2001

Component	*Population*	*Population in percentage*
Denizens with offspring	704,488	30.71
Native tribal population (Kuki and Naga ethnic communities)	670,782	29.24
Native Meitei and other ethnic communities	918,626	40.05
Total	**2,293,896**	**100.00**

Source: United Committee Manipur (2005)

it has happened in Assam or Tripura. Whether the clash between Kuki and Naga communities in the early 1990s is treated as a conflict between migrants and native populations require deeper and further investigations.

It is difficult to imagine how such an underdeveloped hinterland like Manipur that has been affected by enduring armed conflict has attracted so many new migrants. Therefore, some of the probable factors influencing the unrestrained entry of new migrants are highlighted below:

Annulment of inner line permit during the early 1950s

The inner line permit, a policy of 'protective discrimination' (*see* Baruah, 2007)[5] that was put in place for the tribal people of India's Northeast was the brainchild of Verrier Elwin who came to India as a Christian missionary during the colonial era and later became a tribal activist. Jawaharlal Nehru's philosophy of tribal development gave birth to the inner line permit in this frontier region. It was indeed a useful tool for protecting the culture and tradition of the indigenous communities settled in what was perceived to be a 'wild region' (Narayan, 2003). However, this tribal policy, which Nehru embarked upon was criticised by most of the unitarist and nationalist sections of the Indian political elites. They argued that the idea of tribal development, i.e. the tribal protective system was focused on the 'exclusion' of tribal people from India's socio-political dispensation, could ultimately lead to the state breaking up (creating the idea of otherness — mainlanders vs. north-easterners) rather than building a robust nation-state (Baruah, 2007; Haokip, 2010).

As the new political elites now realised the economic opportunities in respect of Southeast and East Asia, they recognised that India's Northeast, once perceived as a living museum for natural wonders and human tribes during the Nehru era, should no longer be kept aloof from the centre's political dispensation. The nationalist feeling among the political elites became intense when the political influence of China began to be felt upon the region and New Delhi slowly began to consider its geo-strategic importance, invoking a real or imagined threat from neighbouring countries. In fact, it was the Chinese invasion of the early-1960s that exposed India's vulnerabilities in the northeastern region. It was the Naga rebels who began to make officials of the post-colonial Indian state anxious. Beginning with the China war, politicians, as well as Indian state bureaucrats, began to see external and internal 'enemies' in this frontier region coming together and constituting a looming threat to national security (Baruah, 2007). In such circumstances, India may not be ready to grant another protective law like the inner line permit to Manipur in the future. Thus, the Indian government was determined to withdraw this by-law as early as the 1950s in order to strengthen the nationalising process in this frontier region. The strategic importance of the frontier region was also highlighted in the annexation of the kingdom of Sikkim in 1975.

Exclusion of Nepali nationals from the term 'foreigner' in India's Foreigner (Protected Areas) Act, 1958 (re-imposed in the late 1970s)

Under Section 1(3) of the Foreigner's (Protected Areas) Act, 1958, the Nepali nationals were exempted from the status of 'foreigner' and allowed to enter into any part of India. Thus, the Nepali nationals soon became an integral part of Manipur's demographic structure. The exemption of Nepali nationals from this by-law was repealed in a 1978 Amendment under Section 1(3), yet the influx has remained constant (United Committee Manipur 2005, 27). The Indo-Nepal Treaty of Peace and Friendship of 1950 could be the main reason for the influx. Article 7 of the treaty allows any citizen of Nepal to move freely in any part of India without a passport or visa. Nepali citizens are also allowed to live or work in any part of India including Manipur.

Ill-defined and poorly protected international boundaries with Myanmar

Unclear demarcation of the international boundary between India and Myanmar has been a great concern to Manipur with regard to its impact on the influx of illegal immigrants. The porous border has also provided a safe haven for insurgent groups and smugglers dealing in arms, drugs and other contraband goods (STRATrisks, 2013).

Occurrence of man-made as well as natural disasters in Bangladesh, Myanmar and Nepal

The Bangladesh liberation war in the early 1970s, ethnic and religious refugees from Myanmar due to dictatorial military junta, victims from constant devastating floods and cyclones in Bangladesh, the unstable government in Nepal, etc. have all contributed to massive influx of migrants to the northeast region including Manipur. Myanmar's decades-long oppression by the military junta led many settlers (including Tamils,

Rohingyas and other ethnic groups (Singh, 2009)[6] from Kachin state) to take shelter in Manipur's border town of Moreh. Reports by local NGOs such as the Federation of Regional Indigenous Societies (FREINDS) and the United Committee Manipur (UCM) revealed that fifty per cent of the total population of the Jiribam subdivision (now Jiribam district) is made up of Bangladeshi migrants. They further claimed that there were around two hundred thousand Nepalese immigrants in Manipur.[7]

Rapid infrastructure development

Rapid infrastructural development has turned India's Northeast including Manipur into an irresistible economic niche[8] resulting in a large-scale influx of migrants that overwhelms native communities. Albeit the Indian state has not followed an overt strategy of 'state sponsoring' or 'state facilitating' (Geiger, 2008), migrants like what the Chinese state does in some of its minority areas (Baruah, 2007), but through the process of modernisation, it certainly provides incentives and opportunities for mobility to this hinterland. This creates a condition to nurture the growth of ethnic identification and ethnic cohesion (Weiner, 1978).

These new migrant communities are mainly labourers who come from the mainland Indian states. The problem starts when they tried to settle in Manipur. Further, it is important to understand that the economic policy of the government has resulted in an unprecedented spread of corruption at all levels of the political establishment. These policies resulted in the superimposition of a corrupt and clientelist class directly subordinated to the orders of the Indian government as overlords of the new state-directed regional economy. The social disruption brought by new developmental policies has also led to a proliferation of armed extortionist groups. All of these activities at the centre engendered much social tension and dissatisfaction within civil societies.[9]

Unwillingness to do menial jobs: Most of the migrant communities take menial jobs and work as domestic helpers, rickshaw pullers, cart pullers, mobile ice-cream or juice vendors, cobblers, barbers, masons etc. as the local people find these jobs unattractive and demeaning.

Counter-insurgency operation in Mizoram

The counter-insurgency operation codenamed 'Operation Jericho' in Mizoram during the mid-1960s to suppress the movement of the Mizo

National Front for a sovereign Mizo nation resulted in many Mizos fleeing to nearby states including Manipur (Tochhawng, 2012). Ethnically Mizos are the kith and kin of the Kukis of Manipur who are mostly settled in Churachandpur district.

Nepalese as the source of income for tribal chiefs

The Nepalese have been known for their bravery since the British period. For this reason, Nepali families are invited by tribal chiefs to look after their huge plots of uninhabited land in the hill districts. In return, the Nepalis utilise the vast hilly lands for grazing as well as for dairy farming. The tribal chiefs, on the other hand, collect 'informal' taxes from the Nepali families.[10] That is how some of the Nepali population are also accommodated into the tribal land.

Political opportunism

Although there is no official documentation on whether the local elected representatives supported undocumented migrants in procuring ration cards, driving licenses, voter identity cards or birth certificates etc., the fact that this is an open secret, as the number of migrants continues to increase (United Committee Manipur, 2005). One shocking case is that the 'Nganukon Refugee Colony' with 820 voters in Kumbi constituency (i.e. Manipur's 29th assembly constituency in Bishnupur district) is a village entirely settled by the Bengalis as well as the Nepalese 'refugees'.[11] But, listing these 'refugee' communities on Manipur's electoral roll (Electoral Office Manipur, 2014) explains everything about the ethics and political principles of the local politicians.

Reports by the United Committee Manipur also reveals that there were around 704,488 migrants, including offspring, as against 670,782 indigenous tribal populations, which is around 31 per cent or about two-thirds of the total population of Manipur — i.e. 2,293,896 (United Committee Manipur, 2005). Further, it was alleged that one of the MLAs of Jiribam was involved in legalising illegal migrants in Manipur (Lisam, 2014).[12]

Preference for non-Manipuri in privately run English medium schools

English education entered Manipur as early as the late-nineteenth century with the establishment of Johnstone M.E. School in 1877 at Imphal under the patronage of King Chandrakirti (*see* Jamini, 2006).[13] There were very few 'English medium' schools until the middle of the twentieth century and most of them were Catholic Mission schools.[14] These schools began to perform very well in local board examinations from the late 1970s and 1980s. Thus, inspired by the success stories of these schools, many 'English medium' schools were set up across the state but run by private local entrepreneurs. However, these entrepreneurs prefer to employ non-Manipuri people, generally mainland Indians and particularly south Indians,[15] to local educated graduates (*see* Figure 10.1, classified advertisements from local newspapers).

Wanted

- Two non-Manipuri Asst. Teachers for lower classes.
- Minimum Qualification: Matriculate
- Scale of pay: Negotiable
- Eligible candidates may apply to the undersigned through the Manager, M/S Ruhini Bandage on or before 23-1-1999
- Interview will be held on 24-1-1999 at 9.30 a.m. at the office chamber of the M/S Ruhini Surgical Bandage Industry, 7/C. Govt. Industrial Estate, Takyel. Tel. No. 222674.

Sd/- Laishram Biren Singh
Administrator
Little Bird English School
Heirok Part II, Khunou

Fig. 10.1: Newspaper clippings of classified advertisements for jobs in Manipur during the 1990s

Source: *The Imphal Free Press*. Date of publication, January 18 and 20, 1999, and United Committee Manipur 2005, 58.

Civil Society Response

By civil society, what we generally understand is the domain that counterbalances the state's fluid policies. It is generally defined as the realm that occupies the space between family and the state. Yet, how much or what civil society has to do with the migration process may be of interest of discussion. Further, the available literature on the role of civil society vis-à-vis migration mainly discusses assistance and aid works or advocacy for migration policy (Thouez, 2004). To the scholars like Robinson (2008), conventional definition of civil society (which occupies the space between family and the state) is somehow contested in the Indian context. For him, associations that are formed on ethnic and religious ascription can also be considered within the realm of modern civil society, as it provides critical reference points for mobilisation and contestation within civil society. On the other hand, scholars like Banerjee (2009) has reservation to consider such groups within the realm of civil society, as such group who attributes on ethnic and religious line often ended up in violent conflict with the outgroup members. Take, for instance, the civil society groups of the northeast region including Manipur are often seen and associated with the confrontation against the migrant groups that normally ended up with violence. Accordingly, Banerjee feels such acts of the so-called 'civil society' made the generic concept blurred and at times difficult to distinguish between 'civility' and the 'incivility.' For her, to place such acts within the concept of civil society has been a point of contention.

Based on the above premise, it is apparent that violence has no justification to be included in the realm of civil society. However, associations or movements that employ peaceful and democratic means of protest may be considered to be a part of civil society. Whatever the case may be, any organisations or associations founded on such ethnic ascription may not be dismissed as primordial or reactive groups from the domain of modern civil society. As Robinson (2008) also argues that it provides a critical reference point for mobilisation, which has a sole character to be considered as civil society. Therefore, for the purpose of this paper, such groups and associations formed on ethnic ascription are considered within the domain of civil society. It may not be wrong to say that many of the civil society organisations of Manipur are also founded on ethnic lines.

Very recently, some sections of the civil societies of Manipur began to be more un-accommodative, often reactive in their approach toward the new migrants and started demanding implementation of inner line permit. It was since the late 1980s that some sections of the civil societies of Manipur began to register a movement demanding for the introduction of the inner line permit to monitor the influx of migrants. It is claimed that the issues of space, resource distributions, citizenship, among other things are the probable reasons behind such movements (Gajananda, 2015).

Plausible reasons behind the inner line permit movement could be many but it is worth noting that the issue of perceived threat to the idea of Manipur intertwined with the political history of Manipur could not be neglected. Manipur's cultural and ethnic identity began to face more difficulties when the migrant communities started advancing claims for indigenous rights over sacred space and resources. For example, the *Tellipati*[16] controversy over land encroachment of a sacred place of the

Meitei community by the migrant communities is a perfect example for invoking such insecurity and hostility (*see Imphal Free Press*, May 20, 2018).

Of course, it is a significant task of the state to make a serious effort to formulate a policy either to incorporate or deter such new migrants before conflict/communal violence can erupt. However, taking such a step to finding that new migrant may cause conflict does not mean that migration has to be discouraged. However, Manipur's pluralism has been put in crisis due to competition over the ownership of both tangible and intangible resources. The proliferation of homeland demands generally paves ways for the perception of out-group members as the 'other', leading to exclusivity and inclusivity. In fact, Manipur's simmering ethnic conflict is often framed as an immigration-derived threat to the presumed homogeneity of their ethnic territory and native democracy.

One of the first democratic protests demanding the detection of undocumented migrants erupted in the early-1980s. The All Manipur Students' Union (AMSU) in alliance with the All Manipur Students' Coordinating Committee (AMSCOC) spearheaded the movement in February 1980 and again in mid-1994 respectively (United Committee Manipur, 2005). The main reason for the protest was the abrupt increase in the decadal population growth rates of 1951–61 and 1961–71 respectively i.e. between 1961 and 1971, the decadal population growth rate (37.53 per cent) was much higher than that of the national decadal growth rate of 24.80 per cent (*see* Table 10.2).

Table 10.2: Decadal population growth rate of India and Manipur from 1931 to 2001

Year	*Population in millions*		*Decennial growth rate (in %)*	
	India	*Manipur*	*India*	*Manipur*
1931	278.98	0.45	11.00	16.04
1941	318.66	0.45	14.22	14.92
1951	361.09	0.58	13.31	12.80
1961	439.02	0.78	21.51	35.04
1971	548.16	1.07	24.80	37.53
1981	683.18	1.42	24.66	32.46
1991	846.30	1.84	23.85	29.29
2001	1027.02	2.29	21.35	24.86

Source: United Committee Manipur (2005).

In both the occasions, the agitation was called off when an agreement was concluded between the Government of Manipur and the AMSU along with the AMSCOC. However, the agreement has yet to be materialised.

Again since the mid-2012 until the time of writing, there has been a fervent movement for the reimplementation of inner line permit in Manipur under the banner, the Joint Committee on Inner Line Permit System (JCILPS), which is a conglomeration of civil societies including local clubs, Meira Paibis (*see* Thangjom, 2013), student organisations, among others. The demand committee allegedly claims that the inner line permit is the only mechanism to monitor the influx of migrants into Manipur. Albeit the legislative assembly of Manipur has in three sessions discussed the issue of inner line permit and passed a Bill, the demand committee has been at loggerheads with the Ministry of Home Affairs of the Government of India, as it may compromise the constitutional rights bestowed in Article No. 19. Further, the said Bill (in its Sub-clauses) was caught up with some ethical and technical issues as it claimed to hurt the sentiment of tribal communities and later sent it to the Standing Committee for further modification.

In spite of setbacks, demand for implementation of inner line permit has gained momentum. The valley-based clubs, women organisations, and others have been steadily taking part in the demand of inner line permit. Very recently, the Indigenous Kuki People's Forum (IKPF) and Zeliangrong Students' Union Barak Valley (ZSUBV) have raised their concern for the imposition of inner line permit while the Kuki Inpi[17] has also joined the movement for the immediate implementation of inner line permit in Manipur. Very recently, the Manipur State Legislative Assembly has tabled and passed the Manipur People Bill 2018, thereby setting the stage for the implementation of the inner line permit in the state.

Demand for Inner Line Permit or *Mayang*-phobia?

One may surely observe in the inner line permit movement that migrants from mainland Indian regions are apparently targeted and often stand at the receiving end including vandalising shops[18] or using derogatory remarks. It is evident from a sort of derogative remark — the *Mayang* used in the anti-migrant narrative (Rameshchandra, 2012; Ningthouja, 2015). *Mayang*, from a historical point of view, are those people who were the inhabitants of the Cachar district of Assam. The former king of Manipur, Kiyamba, who came into contact with the Cacharis in AD 1504, called them *Mayang(s)* (Kabui 1991). For most of the people of Manipur today, however, *Mayang* (though it was the terminology used for the Cacharis during the sixteenth to nineteenth centuries) has nothing to do with people from Cachar.

Some Manipuri scholars try to interpret *Mayang* as those people who are non-native, non-Manipuri or any individuals who are foreign to native Manipur. However, it is difficult to accept this interpretation because contemporary Manipuri society would not call a Chinese, a Thai national or a Burmese migrant a *Mayang*. For most of the people of Manipur today *Mayang* are indisputably those people who have sharp features (broader eyes, sharper nose), brown skin colour etc. — i.e. broadly the people from mainland India.

Also by reviewing the reports of the United Committee Manipur as well as local newspapers, one can observe that the inner line permit agitation has been tending to give negative signals — *Mayang*-phobic and Meitei-centric agitation (Ningthouja, 2015; Rameshchandra, 2012). If the agitation is about checking the influx of illegal migrants to Manipur, then the inner line demand committee should also address the illegal Burmese Chin-Kuki migrants who can easily intrude into the state. Of course, some illegal migrants are kith and kin of some of the ethnic communities in Manipur. To campaign against such groups tends to divide people into communal lines that can create further tension among the fragile ethnic set up of the state (Singh, 2009).

Mention may be made here that the erstwhile kingdom of Manipur tackled the issue of migration successfully without much ado. The society was also able to integrate people who came to the kingdom. The main reason could be the scarcity of manpower due to the constant wars with neighbouring kingdoms, particularly the Burmese. Another reason could be the abundance of resources. There was a time when Muslims who were war captives were offered Manipuri/Meitei women and assigned appropriate Meitei surnames. Similarly, there is the case of Brahmins who migrated from the west — '*nongchup haram*' (western gateway). So there was no problem with migrants in the erstwhile kingdom.

Of course, there might certainly be a reason why Manipuri society tends to see the migrants of the mainland as the prime threat to the demographic structure of Manipur. In fact, the political history of Manipur plays a significant role in shaping such un-accommodative attitude and often reflected in their approach. Theories of nationalising state (Connor, 1972; Brubaker, 1996) and developmental paradigm (that attracts or facilitates immigrants) can help us to demystify Manipuri civil society vs. *Mayang* in inner line permit demand discourse. Because nationalising the problematic space either through state-facilitate or state-sponsored settlement (Geiger,

2008) or through coercive measures certainly evoke homeostatic nationalism (Conversi, 1995) in order to safeguard themselves from any neo-colonising entity. As such, *Mayang*-phobia can be seen as a part of (homeostatic) nationalism that focuses precisely on the process of reaction against the state's nation-building approaches. Take, for instance, the Chinese state-sponsored migration as a tool of nation-building in some of its minority frontier areas aroused discontentment. The Indian state albeit not follow such an overt strategy, but certainly attracts migrants through such nationalising and developmental models received with mixed feelings.

Detection and Deportation of Illegal Migrants

As per the agreement that was signed between AMSU, AMSCOC and the Government of Manipur in 1994, the government agreed to undertake immediate steps to detect illegal migrants based on the electoral roll of 1948, in which the process of identifying illegal migrants followed the provisions of the Foreigner Act 1946 (United Committee Manipur, 2005). Yet, such action has never been carried out. Besides, the detection and repatriation of illegal foreigners based on the 1948 electoral roll becomes more complicated or almost impossible when the provisions of India's Citizenship Act of 1955 are taken into consideration. In fact, the Citizenship Act has been a stumbling block to formulate such policy. As per section 2(1)(b) of the Citizenship Act of 1955 defines an illegal immigrant as those people who enter into Indian territory:

(a) Without a valid passport or other travel documents and such other document or authority as may be prescribed by or under any law in that behalf; or
(b) With a valid passport or other travel documents and such other document or authority as may be prescribed by or under any law in that behalf but remains therein beyond the permitted period of time.

Section 3 of the Citizenship Act of 1955 (acquisition of citizenship) says that,

(a) A person born in India on or after 26 January 1950, but before 1 July 1987, is a citizen of India by birth irrespective of the nationality of his/her parents.
(b) A person born in India on or after 1 July 1987, but before 3 December 2004, is considered a citizen of India by birth if either

of his/her parents is a citizen of India at the time of his/her birth.

(c) A person born in India on or after 3 December 2004, is considered a citizen of India by birth if both the parents are citizens of India or one of the parents is a citizen of India and the other is not an illegal migrant at the time of his/her birth.

Section 5 (4) further says that any minor child can be registered as a citizen of India, if the central government is satisfied that there are 'special circumstances' justifying such registration. These above-mentioned provisions of the Citizenship Act together with the fact that most immigrants who entered Indian Territory have not followed the legal process to become Indian citizens complicate the issue of identifying the illegal immigrants. Further, political consensus on the issue of migration has also been long overdue. In such a situation, there emerged an issue of ethnic tension between the natives and immigrants or even amongst the natives. There are further complexities surrounding the identification of illegal foreigners. The detection of illegal immigrants has turned out to be a big problem for the government, as some illegal immigrants are kith and kin of some of the ethnic communities in Manipur. To campaign against these illegal immigrants tends to divide people into communal lines that may create more tension among the fragile multi-ethnic society.

Conclusion

It is evident that the erstwhile kingdom of Manipur used to have its own migration policy in place that helped the kingdom to build a common culture shared by various ethnic groups which helped mitigate much of the possible ethnic tensions. Today, the territory of Manipur that acquires a vital geostrategic location that lies on the trade routes of Southeast Asia is indeed becoming an inevitable business for India. Therefore, it is quite necessary for the Indian state to settle down the long-drawn insurgency movement. The zealous developmental mission that had directed to uplift this remote backward region is not bad in itself. The issue lies on filling up the frontier peripheries with migrants that have not borne the full signature of the national community to nationalise the frontier space. It would ultimately have a detrimental effect on governance, migrant communities and native people. Therefore, the centre's inability to regulate a comprehensive migration policy is a serious cause of concern. *Mayang*-phobia comes in the interstice as a part of Manipuri nationalism that focuses precisely on the process of reaction against the state's nation-building approaches. In fact, *Manyang*-phobia can be argued as the frustration amongst the Manipuri society manifest against the state's nationalising policy. Mayang is made a soft target of such frustrations.

With regard to the debate surrounding inner line permit, it is worth noting the experience of the state of Nagaland, which has had the inner line permit since its inception but also has a huge number of migrants particularly in and around the towns of Dimapur, Kohima and Mokokchung. In addition, a new social category has emerged which is popularly known as Semiya — a cross breed between the Sema tribe of Nagaland and Bangladeshi Muslims. Thus, it is imperative to consider whether the re-implementation of inner line permit in Manipur would really keep a check on the unchecked migrants/non-Manipuris or whether it would meet with the same fate as in Nagaland.

Notes

1. Manipur become a part of Indian Union in 1949.
2. The inner line permit is an apparatus for checking the influx of any non-native populations into the northeastern region and some other selected regions of India during the colonial period. In 1950, the permit system was repealed in the state of Manipur. However, the permit still exists in Arunachal Pradesh, Mizoram and Nagaland. For further details, *see* Appendix IV of the report of United Committee Manipur (2005), pp 127-134.
3. Meitei is particularly mentioned instead of all the ethnic communities of Manipur because the agitation for (re)-implementation of inner line permit is mainly confined within the valley districts.
4. See, '*Migrants insecure after rebel group's 'quit notice'*, *The Times of India*, September 8, 2012.
5. A policy of non-intervention or exclusion that is enforced by a provision called the Bengal Eastern Frontier Regulation, 1873, which restricts property ownership by non-tribal in the tribal states of Northeast India which on the other hand, contradicts the constitutional right of free movement of being an Indian citizen. For further details, *see* Baruah, S., (2007), 51–53.
6. The case of Burmese Kuki migrants has been a complicated issue as they share their ethnicity with some of the ethnic groups of Manipur. *Also see* Singh, M. A., (2009).
7. *See* 'Migrants Outnumber Meiteis: ILP demand to gain momentum set July 11 deadline', *The Hueiyenlanpao*, June 27, 2013.
8. India's Northeast has been designated as a 'special category' region. The North Eastern Council receives 90 per cent of the plan assistance as a grant and 10 per cent as a loan, while other Indian states receive only 30 per cent as a grant and 70 per cent as loan. *See* Bhaumik, S. (2009), p. 232.

9. The building of mastodontic dams and road/communication infrastructure, the expansion of extractive activities and mining in disputed areas (including forced land grabbing) and other activities at huge cost to Manipur's environment and culture have resulted into adverse effects including the displacement of thousands of people. This has led to a spiral of social unrest and state repression affecting the harmonious coexistence of the entire region.
10. An interview with a Nepali grazing family at Mayaiching Khongjai hill of Senapati district, Manipur.
11. Refugees from the Bangladesh Liberation War of 1971.
12. *See* Lisam, K. 2014. 'What should the State Government do for implementation of the Inner Line Permit System in Manipur?', *The Sangai Express*, August 11.
13. British political agents such as Captain Gordon, Major General W.E. Nuthall and R. Brown all tried to introduce western (English) education during the early 1870s, but they all failed, as the people of Manipur had no interest in western education. For details, *see* Jamini, (2006), p. 30.
14. Pettigrew School, a Christian mission school established in 1895, Don Bosco High School, Imphal, a Catholic Mission school established in 1957 were prominent Christian mission schools in Manipur.
15. The literacy rate of Kerala has fared very well in India's education index with more than 90 per cent for many years. Many graduates from Kerela somehow also reached Manipur during the 1980s and 1990s in search of jobs and they mostly found jobs in these booming 'English medium' schools in Manipur.
16. Tellipati is one neighbourhood mostly settled by Bihari migrants.
17. Kuki Inpi is the apex organisation of the Kuki people.
18. 'JCILPS vandalises fruit shops adjacent to Bhairodan school', *The People's Chronicle*, May 2, 2018.

References

Andreas, P. 2003. Redrawing the Line: Borders and Security in the Twenty-First Century, *International Security*, 28 (2), 78-111.

Arango, J. 2000. Explaining Migration: A Critical View, *International Social Science Journal*, 52 (165), 283-296.

Banerjee, M. 2009. Civil Society and Violence in India's Northeast, *Journal of Civil Society*, V(2), 151-167.

Baruah, S. 2007. *Durable Disorder: Understanding the Politics of Northeast India*. New Delhi: Oxford University Press.

Bhaumik, S. 2009. *Troubled Periphery*. New Delhi: Sage Publications India Pvt Ltd.

Brubaker, R. 1996. Nationalising States in the old, 'New Europe' and the new, *Ethnic and Racial Studies*, 19(2), 411-437.

Connor, W. 1972. Nation-Building or Nation-Destroying?, *World Politics*, 24(3), 319-355,

Conversi, D. 1995. Reassessing current theories of nationalism: Nationalism as boundary maintenance and creation, *Nationalism and Ethnic Politics*, 1(I), 73-85.

Electoral Office Manipur. 2014. *Electoral Rolls*. Imphal: Chief Electoral Officer, Manipur.

Gajananda, K. 2015, July 28. *ILPS And Indigenous Peoples Rights: Manipur, The Imphal Free Press*: http://www.ifp.co.in/page/items/27710/ilps-and-indigenous-peoples-rights-manipur/. (accessed 21 June 2018).

Geiger, D. 2008. *Frontier Encounter: Indigenous Communities and Settlers in Asia and Latin America*, (ed.). Copenhagen: IWGIA.

Haokip, T. 2010. India's Northeast Policy: Continuity and Change, *Man and Society: A Journal of North East Studies*, VII.

Jamini. 2006. *Education in Manipur*. Imphal: Rai Pravina Brothers.

Kabui, G. 1991. *History of Manipur* (Vol. 1). New Delhi: National Publishing House.

Robinson, M. 2008. Civil Society and Ideological Contestation in India, in C. Elliott, *Civil Society and Democracy: A Reader* (pp. 356-376). New Delhi: Oxford University Press.

Narayan, J. 2003. *Nation Building in India*. Varanasi: Brahmanand Navachetna Prakashan.

Ningthouja, M. 2015. 'Lines Between 'Us' and 'Them' in Manipur: Genesis of Mayangphobia and ILPS Movement till August 2015, *Eastern Quarterly*, 11(III&IV), pp. 101-123.

Ninna, Nyberg Sørensen, *et al.* 2003. 'Migration, Development and Conflict: State-of-the-Art Overview', in Nicholas Var Hear and Ninna Nyberg Sørensen (ed.), *The Migration-Development Nexus* (pp. 5-50). Geneva: United Nations and the International Organization for Migration.

Rameshchandra, N. 2012, July 25. *Some Comments on the Discourse of ILP*, The E-pap. www.e-pao.net: http://e-pao.net/epSubPageExtractor.asp?src=education.Scientific_Papers. (accessed July 28, 2012).

Ravenstein, E.G. 1985. The Laws of Migration, *Journal of the Statistical Society*, 48 (2), 167-235.

Singh, M.A. 2009. *A Study on Illegal Immigration into North-East India: The Case of Nagaland*. New Delhi: Institute for Defence Studies and Analysis.

Sjaastad, L.A. 1962. The Costs and Returns of Human Migration, *Journal of Political Economy*, 70(5), 80-93.

STRATrisks. 2013. 'Eastern India new smuggling hub', *Stratrisks*, 27 July.

Thangjom, L. 2013. The Role of Meira Paibi in Bringing about Social Change in the Manipuri Society: an Analysis, *Journal of Social Welfare and Management*, 4, 235-239.

Thouez, C. 2004. *The role of civil society in the migration policy debate*. New York: Global Commission on International Migration.

Tochhawng, J.V. 2012. *The Mizo Uprising: Assam Assembly Debates on the Mizo Movement, 1966-1971*. Newcastle: Cambridge Scholars Publishing.

United Committee Manipur. 2005. *Influx of Migrants into Manipur: A Threat to the Indigenous Ethnic People*. Imphal: UCM, 127-134.

Valeriano, B. 2009. When Does Migration Lead to Interstate Conflict? *International Studies Association and Western Political Science*, Chicago: University of Illinois, 1-22.

Weiner, M. 1978. *Sons of Soil: Migration and Ethnic Conflict in India*. New Delhi: Oxford University Press.

11

Why Inner Line Permit and Sixth Schedule?

A Discussion Drawn from Experiences in Jiribam District of Manipur

Immanuel Zarzosang Varte

If we can sit down, then surely we can lie down *(Boiteparlegumaite pare)*
— An old Bangladeshi saying

After prolonged agitation and negotiations for implementation of Inner Line Permit System (ILPS) in Manipur, the controversial Manipur Regulation of Visitors, Tenants and Migrant Workers (MRVTMW) Bill of 2015 has been withdrawn by the government. However, the demand for implementation of the Inner Line Permit (ILP) continues with a resurgence reminiscent of the incident that took place in 2015 possible in the near future.

Like its predecessor, the current government is also in a political tight-rope over this issue as the ILP was also allegedly used as a campaign tool by it to woo voters. However, almost a year after the Bharatiya Janata Party (BJP) came to power in Manipur for the first time, the ILP issue in Manipur is no way nearer to its conclusion or solution. Now, with public pressure mounting and with continued denial and excuses giving more political benefits and advantages to those critical of the present government, the BJP led government has been forced into an awkward back-stand position and trying to ease these pressures by taking up certain steps, culturally and politically sensitive, to curb non-natives from illegally entering and settling in the state. As this effort has its epicentre in Jiribam, the paper will focus on the illegal migration issue in Jiribam.

Why ILP by the Meiteis and Sixth Schedule by the Tribals?

The idea of Meiteis being threatened and marginalised is very real even though it may sound farfetched to some. Just because a certain community is demographically a majority in a certain area does not mean that they are impervious or safe from both external and internal (even though external is often more in such cases) discriminations, oppressions or marginalisation from other bigger and more dominant communities. This is especially true for the Meiteis, who, even though may be the majority community in Manipur presently, and this is changing rapidly, are a very small minority when compared against other non-tribal communities of India. Given this, they, as well as other small tribal communities of Manipur, have every reason to fear and feel threatened especially when one takes into account their own rapid rise in population, migration from outside and within the state to the valley vis-à-vis fast decreasing available land and other resources in the valley area coupled with the increasing non-Manipuri population as per the 2011 Census[1] and their increasing influence in the state politically, economically and socially.[2] It is also a fact that the valleys of Manipur, the main source of food for the State, are being overpopulated and available resources over-utilised and strained almost beyond capacity. This may be one of the main reasons why the government is so keen on reclaiming more wetlands — to make more space, though this policy is ill-reasoned and extremely damaging in the long run. Therefore, the demand for ILPS is legitimate and its implementation in the State especially urgent.

For many tribal areas that do not come under the hill administration such as in Jiribam, the issue of migration is also a very real and urgent problem and which ILPS may be able to address.

While discussing ILP which is predominantly demanded by the Meitei community, mention is required of a parallel and almost similar demand by the hill tribes, which is a 6th Schedule under the Indian Constitution. The Central Government recently sent a letter to the Government of Manipur regarding implementation of 6th Schedule in the hills of Manipur, the hill districts are also in a state of mixed expectations. In spite of the outward facade of bonhomie, the game of thrones being played out among the myriad tribal communities in the hills of Manipur may be much more than meets the eye. Many times, smaller tribes find themselves sandwiched between two competing groups and being torn apart in the process. While the 6th Schedule can be a boon, it can also be a curse for some unless proper mechanisms to distribute benefits equally are in place. The 6th

Schedule is also akin to a double-edged sword indeed.[3]

Nonetheless, notwithstanding such apprehensions, 6th Schedule in the hill districts of Manipur will certainly be instrumental in solving several long-standing tribal issues in the state and its implementation will also certainly help to further safeguard indigenous peoples' lands and identities. There are, however, some suspicions among the hill tribes that the Government of Manipur is trying to sidetrack a response to the implementation of 6th Schedule in the Hills and the demand for ILPS at this juncture is actually conveniently helping it to do this as the latter appears to be more 'pressing matters' than the former. The silence of the valley populace, and even open opposition from some quarters, to the issue of implementation of 6th Schedule in the hills of Manipur does not help in assailing these fears or the feelings of being ignored. To make the climate of distrust worse, there are also suspicion among some intelligentsia that the demand for ILPS in the State also has the twin objective of lending more strength and legitimacy to the Meitei ST demand.

Migrant Issue in Jiribam

The history of Jiribam mainly begins with the colonial rule. A number of tribes and people of other religions began to migrate to the riverside area in the beginning of the 19th century. The Jiri River was very famous during this era and Jiribam was a major trade centre. The entire area was then ruled by Maharaja Churachand Singh from 1891–1941, who was then a minor. In the year 1907, the Manipur State Durbar was established to assist the Maharaja in the administration of the area. His son, Maharaja Budhachandra Singh ruled the area from 1941-1955. In 1940, Jiribam became a Mauzar and in 1950, the office of the Mauzardar of Jiribam was converted into a S.D.C. office.[4] Jiribam existed as a Sub-Division first under Tamenglong and then Imphal East till the mid 2016 when it became a full-fledged Revenue district. During the last Manipur Assembly election in 2017, one candidate belonging to a non-tribal- non-Meitei community won thereby creating history in as far as Jiribam is concerned.

As of 2011 India census, Jiribam district had a total population of 43,838, out of which 22,539 were males while 21,299 were females. In 2011, there were total 8,355 families residing in Jiribam. The Average Sex Ratio of Jiribam was 945.

As per Census 2011, out of total population, 16.8 per cent people lived in urban areas while 83.2 per cent lived in the rural areas. The average literacy rate in urban areas was 88.8 per cent while that in rural areas was 72.5 per cent. Also the Sex Ratio of urban areas in Jiribam was 920 while that of rural areas was 950.

The total literacy rate of Jiribam was 75.43 per cent. The male literacy rate was 69.39 per cent and the female literacy rate was 56.48 per cent.

Jiribam District Data

As per the Population Census 2011 data, following are some quick facts about Jiribam District.

	Total	*Male*	*Female*
Children (Age 0-6)	7,158	3,642	3,516
Literacy	75.43%	69.39%	56.48%
Scheduled Caste	7,425	3,862	3,563
Scheduled Tribe	5,490	2,818	2,672
Illiterate	16,170	6,900	9,270

Caste-wise Population – Jiribam District

Schedule Caste (SC) constituted 16.9 per cent while Schedule Tribe (ST) was 12.5 per cent of total population in Jiribam District.

	Total	*Male*	*Female*
Scheduled Caste	7,425	3,862	3,563
Scheduled Tribe	5,490	2,818	2,672

Religion-wise Population – Jiribam District

Religion	*Total*	*Percent*	*Male*	*Female*
Hindu	21,323	(48.64)	11,065	10,258
Muslim	14,934	(34.07)	7,592	7,342
Christian	5,846	(13.34)	3,012	2,834
Sikh	13	(0.03)	10	3
Buddhist	27	(0.06)	12	15
Jain	6	(0.01)	1	5
Other Religion	1,652	(3.77)	828	824
No Religion Specified	37	(0.08)	19	18

With National Highway-37 and the railway (now part of Trans-Asian Railway) passing through it[5], Jiribam, which is located in the westernmost part of Manipur, is an important and crucial town bordering Cachar district of Assam has been an entry point for goods, foodgrains, people and many other things for decades. It is also known as the "Western Gate" of Manipur. Jiribam is currently inhabited by various communities—Meiteis, Meitei-Pangan, Bengali-Muslims, Bengali-Hindus, Nagas, Thadou-Kuki, Kabui/Rongmei, Tangkhul, Hmar, Bishnupriya, Nepali etc. of which the Meitei dominates while Hmar is the dominating tribal group. It is one of the fastest growing towns in Manipur.[6]

Taking advantage of the porous International Border between India and Bangladesh at Cachar District of Assam, large scale illegal migrants pose a serious threat to the demographic, socio-political, socio-economic and environmental balance and stability in Jiribam *per se* and Manipur in general. While it is historically known that Jiribam being in close proximity with Cachar District of Assam always had a large non-local population, illegal migrants from Bangladesh and migrants from neighbouring Cachar have increasingly become a serious demographic issue — more so the former. Unfortunately, the allegations that some local political and community leaders along with the bureaucracy have been providing refuge to migrants, help them obtain certain documents to make them non-local and using them as vote banks might hold a more truth than the eye can see.

With a sudden and phenomenal increase in the number of people unable to speak Hindi, Meitei, English or other indigenous dialects except their own[7] during the past 10-15 years and then settling/encroaching on lands that are often prime agricultural lands — be it wet agricultural or jhum, there is a serious and acute strain on lands available for cultivation. With an already depleted resource available to feed the existing original population, large scale migrations are straining lands and other resources in Jiribam. Furthermore, there is also a real fear of indigenous peoples' socio-political and socio-economic rights and advantages being threatened.

The whole demographic balance is now so confused and imbalanced that it has become a census enumerator's nightmare.

It is alarming to note that many tribal lands and villages hitherto having names specific to the tribes living in that area are now being changed into non-local names and dominated by the same. Below is an example of the names of some villages under Jiribam and Pherzawl districts of Manipur many of which were inhabited by Hmar, Naga and Kuki tribes now having non-local names and dominated by the same[8].

Manipur government takes steps to check entry of illegal migrants from Assam

By PTI. Published: 04th January 2018 02:10 PM

Last Updated: 04th January 2018 03:07 PM

IMPHAL: The Manipur government is taking measures to prevent a possible spillover of illegal migrants into the state in view of the publication of the first draft of the "National Register of Citizens" (NRC) in Assam.

The NRC, first prepared in 1951, is being updated in Assam under supervision of the Supreme Court, to weed out illegal migrants. The first draft of the updated version was published on December 31.

Special teams, led by officers of the rank of Assistant Commandant or Additional Senior SPs, have been deployed at Jiribam Babupara Bazar and along the Barak river bordering Mizoram, the Manipur Police said in a statement today.

The Barak originates in Manipur, flows through Mizoram and Assam and enters Bangladesh, where it forks into the Surma and Kushiyara rivers.

Special police teams have also been deployed at Mao Gate in Senapati district bordering Nagaland and the Tamei-Haflong road in Tamenglong district bordering Assam to check the entry of migrants into the state, the press release read.

Source: http://www.newindianexpress.com/nation/2018/jan/04/manipur-government-takes-steps-to-check-entry-of-illegal-migrants-from-assam-1744330.html

The Government of Manipur is trying to stop migrant illegally entering the State. As such, the present police drive at Jiribam is definitely timely. It is, of course, good not only in demographic sense but also in all the possible political senses. The stopping of 100 migrants from adjacent districts of Assam at Jiribam is just fire-fighting mechanism. This mechanism is not enough for solving the real problem and for avoiding Assam-like riots in future Manipur. The general feeling in the State is that there may be many more that settled in villages or formed villages of their own. At present, the need of the hour is to identify all the illegal migrants and to take necessary legal actions.[9] One of the hurdles to such identification is the base year — would it be 1951, 1971, 1981 or 1991? There was a debate over the base year when All Manipur Students' Union (AMSU) spearheaded the anti-foreigner agitation in 1980-81. The student body demanded to take 1951 as base year of foreigner identification; the Government of Manipur suggested that the base year should be 1971. There were two agreements between AMSU and Government of India. Nothing, however, came out. Over two decades, the issue was kept on hold.

Meantime, while it is prudent and crucial to take immediate steps to curb illegal migrations to the state from other areas/regions and conducting intensive identification drives to help in the process, the continuation of identification of foreign origin migrants needs a proper policy, a Standard Operating Procedure, because it involves various human rights and citizenship issues, and undoubtedly in some cases citizenships of their children born in Manipur, question of female spouses who are Manipuris and many more. It demands larger social discussion on these issues; otherwise the present drive will not give a permanent solution to the snowballing effects of illegal migration.[10]

Conclusion

It is in this complex and vitiated context that the current movements for an ILPS and 6th Schedule in the State of Manipur may offer a rare opportunity to kill many birds with one stone! However, the process, methods and outcome of these movements need careful and critical appraisal so that pre-existing suspicions, rivalries and even hostilities are not perpetuated. It is unfortunate that there have been very few consultations between the tribal and Meitei leaders in Manipur except for sporadic and chance meetings that never really afford opportunities to indepthly know each other's issues and concerns. There is a great and urgent need for a soul-baring dialogue among the peoples of Manipur to ensure the protection of our lands and heritage for our future generations. This is indeed a huge responsibility. After all, the ILPS and the 6th Schedule are both not meant to be a permanent legislation. They are both interim measures till a uniform and equitable deal is eventually in place; a deal that is in keeping with international standards of human rights.

It may be that because of some ill-conceived politics, the climate of mistrust, reservations and apprehensions that exist between the peoples of Manipur may just be misconceptions but they are deeply entrenched misconceptions nonetheless. Therefore, sincere efforts to clear such misconceptions have to be seriously pursued. While ignorance may be bliss, ignorance is also often the source of tension, conflicts and strained relations. As such, is the present generation of Manipur prepared for this role? This a most crucial question yet to be answered but yes, which can be answered, if there is a unified cultural and political will.

Notes

1. As per 2011 census, Meiteis are 7.5 lakh, Tribals 6.7 lakh, non-Manipuris 7.4 lakh. If the Scheduled Castes are excluded, the Meiteis trail non-Manipuris by around 13,000.
2. *See* Immanuel Varte, "Manipur urgently needs Inner Line Permits – but not if they deepen the hostility among communities", 7 August 2015. http://scroll.in/

article/745782/manipur-urgently-needs-inner-line-permits-but-not-if-they-deepen-the-hostility-among-communities.

3. *See* Immanuel Varte "Manipur's dilemma: Can there be hills without valleys?" 18 September, 2015. http://scroll.in/article/755822/manipurs-dilemma-can-there-be-hills-without-valleys.
4. *See* https://ipfs.io/ipfs/QmXoypizjW3WknFiJnKLwHCnL72vedxjQkDDP1mXWo6uco/ wiki/ Jiribam.html
5. Jiribam Rail Station is the first and last railhead for Northeast Frontier Railroad (NFR) in Manipur so far.
6. https://en.wikipedia.org/wiki/Jiribam
7. Many tribals living in remote areas of Manipur are not able to speak Meitei, Hindi or English except their own. However, this is understandable due to their isolation and lack of contact with the outside world. The non-Meitei and non-tribal peoples in Jiribam, on the other hand, professing to be natives of Jiribam and not able to speak Hindi, English or Meitei other than their own dialect is proof that they are just recent inhabitants as Jiribam is neither remote due to good connectivity nor ethnically closed due to its highly mixed population of Indian Bengalis, Meiteis, tribals, etc.
8. This is not to say that the non-Meitei and non-tribal inhabitants of these villages are illegal migrants as many of them have been living there for decades and may actually have been there even longer than many others. This is rather to point out the drastic demographic change in and around Jiribam due to increasing Bengali population.

Sl. No.	*Village No. & Name*	*Sl. No.*	*Village No. & Name*
1.	No. 12(l) Jakuradhor Pt.(l)	14.	No. 23-Tupidhor
2.	No. 12(l)-Jakuradhor Pt(ll)	15.	No. 27(a)-Chowdhurikhal
3.	No. 12(A)-Bhumikpara	16.	No. 7(B)-Chotobekra
4	No. 12(B)-Modhopur	17.	No. 9-Bhutangkhal
5.	No. 12(C)-Durgapur	18.	No. 18-Lama Bhutangkhal
6.	No. 21-Harinagar	19.	No. 11-Borobekra
7.	No. 31-Narayanpur	20.	No. 11(B)-Goakhal
8.	No. 31-Kotakhul	21.	No. 26-Jatrapur
9.	No. 27(B)-Borokhal	22.	No. 27(l)-Sibapurikhal
10.	No. 27(ll)-Kasurbali	23.	No. 11(C)-Nutur Lalpani
11.	No. 11(A)-Nungsek Punji	24.	No. 11(D)-Phaileinpunji
12.	No. 9(A)-Mulkhangthol	25	No. 9(B)-Puthikhal
13.	No. 34-Henchungpunji	26.	No. 32-Terathol

9. Please read further M.C. Arun's "Identification of Illegal Migrants: New Challenges" http://www.ifp.co.in/page/items/9196/9196-identification-of-illegal-migrants-new-challenges/
10. Please read further M.C. Arun's "Identification of Illegal Migrants: New Challenges" http://www.ifp.co.in/page/items/9196/9196-identification-of-illegal-migrants-new-challenges/

12

Inner Line Permit System

Battlelines in Manipur[1]

Dhiren A. Sadokpam

One thing any perceptive observers would notice is the overlapping of identity politics with the rights discourse. What is even more interesting is that all the arguments citing historical commissions and omissions have centered on demand for protective rights. While doing so, both the opponents and supporters of the inner line permit system as devised by the state government of Manipur seem to have fallen trap to a self-imposed restriction and the overarching legal framework. Along the way, the finer details of separating the legal component from the political core have been blurred, rendering the current dispensation virtually helpless.

The 'demand and protest' for and against the implementation of a mechanism for the protection of indigenous communities of Manipur seem to have further compounded the prolonged turmoil witnessed in the state. The unfolding situation has also further deepened the discourse surrounding the idea and praxis of legislation with opposing groups clamouring for protective laws. The author looks at the contours of state response to the demand for the implementation of the inner line permit system in the state.

In line with the longstanding demand for the implementation of the inner line permit system, the Joint Committee on Inner Line Permit System (JCILPS[2]), a civil society group, has been spearheading a movement that seeks the passage of a Bill by the Manipur legislative assembly. The state government has consistently turned a blind eye to the demand. In 2011, a motion was moved in the assembly on the issue. This follows the argument put up by the JCILPS that since the inner line permit was implemented in Nagaland, Mizoram and Arunachal Pradesh; the same should be applied in Manipur as well. The JCILPS's demand is based on the premise that unabated inflow of migrants into Manipur has serious adverse economic, social and political consequences on the body politics of the indigenous peoples.

As part of its campaign for the implementation of the inner line permit, the JCILPS has also invoked historical narrative to prove its points of view. It has elaborately argued that such a mechanism is not a new regulation in Manipur. It stated that in 1901, during the British dispensation and before the merger of Manipur with the Union of India, the state had devised an effective system of 'controlling the entry of foreigners (non-Manipuris)' called the Permit or Passport system (*see* Tarapot, 2003; Chishti, 2005, 134). According to the JCILPS, Indians coming from other parts of the country were called 'foreigners in the terminology of Manipur administration'. The said permit system was brought under the Foreigners Department on November 1, 1931. If the 'foreigners' wished to visit Manipur, they were required to take prior permission from the then Durbar and had to pay certain fees. Such permit system apparently served two important purposes: controlled and regulated the influx of non-Manipuris; and it formed an important mechanism for the generation of revenue for the then state of Manipur.

In this regard, others have also argued that the demand for the mechanism has its roots in the colonial period. The impact of 'foreigners' during the period also indirectly led to the women's uprising that Manipur saw in 1939. The control of the local economy and market 'by a handful of non-local traders' who had established a monopoly impacted the lives of the people in Manipur. "Towards the end of the Second World War, questions were raised on how to check the increasing influence of 'outsiders' in the economic affairs of Manipur. As a response to the public pressure, the Manipur State Durbar Resolution No. 14 of December 23, 1946, resolved to formally screen the entry of outsiders and visitors to Manipur".[3] The move of Manipur State Durbar as far as regulating the entry of 'foreigners' also coincided with the British India government's initiative to bring in a significant number of princely states closer to the Indian Union through the Standstill Agreement and Instrument of Accession in the mid of 1947 (*see* Arun, 2001).

The JCILPS had also been pointing out that in 1948, the Government of India had "officially approved retention of the permit system in Manipur, vide G.E.D Walker, Advisor to the Governor of Assam, letter No. 120147/C-26-27 dated January 1, 1948" (*see* JCILPS, 2012). Himmat Singh, the then Chief Commissioner on November 18, 1950, abolished this permit system, "allowing free entry, the unchecked influx of outsiders from other states" (*see* JCILPS, 2012). This permit system prohibited any foreigner to acquire or purchase land in Manipur. The JCILPS further argued that though Manipur's landmass comprised of '90 per cent hills', the question of implementing the Bengal Eastern Frontier Regulation, 1973 did not arise since Manipur was a princely state (*see* JCILPS, 2012).

Inner Line Permit System

The inner line permit system is based on the Bengal Eastern Frontier Regulation, 1873.[4] The regulation was made under the Government of India Act, 1870 and Government of India Act, 1915, in the then province of Assam. Even after independence, the regulation, which was incipiently intended to maintain peace while governing over some districts on the then Eastern Frontier of Bengal, was made applicable in parts of present-day Northeast India. The regulation was originally applicable to the districts of Kamrup, Darrang, Nowgong, Sibsagar, Lakhimpur (now in Assam), Khasi, Jaintia and Garo Hills (now in Meghalaya), Naga Hills (now Nagaland) and Cachar (Assam). Later the regulation was extended to Nagaland, Arunachal Pradesh, and Mizoram.

The same regulation stated that any person entering the prescribed and notified 'inner line' has to obtain a pass/permit. Further, the holder of such a pass/permit shall, in breach of any restriction or condition, be liable 'to imprisonment' or fine or both. After India had achieved Independence, there have been necessary omissions concerning what were 'British subjects or any class of British subjects'. Section 7 of the regulation also specified that it was against the law for those outside the 'inner line' to acquire any 'interest in land or the product of land'. In the opinion of the JCILPS, the introduction of the permit would eventually safeguard the 'interest' of the land and protect its people.

Prolonged Turmoil

Manipur is embroiled in a prolonged turmoil as the mass agitation for the permit intensified in 2015. In response to the demand of the people, the state government finally had to act. The Manipur Regulation of Visitors, Tenants and Migrant Workers (MRVT&MW) Bill, 2015 was introduced in the state assembly. While a section of the people hoped, this would bring in a tangible resolution to the imbroglio; the JCILPS rejected the Bill. Since the passing of the Bill on March 16, 2015, the valley areas were virtually placed under a deceptive calm. The then Chief Minister O. Ibobi Singh introduced the bill on March 13, 2015. Just a day before the Bill was passed, the writing on the wall was clear. The JCILPS rejected it. The JCILPS had accused the government of attempting to protect migrants or visitors rather than the interests of the indigenous communities. It alleged that the Bill was focused on safety measures for 'outsiders' visiting the state. Moreover, rather than empowering authorities to deport transgressing 'outsiders', the Bill focused on punishing indigenous landowners who failed to follow the regulations. It alleged that the Bill was drafted only to please the Government of India and was not in favour of the people of the state. It vowed that it would not cow down to either pressure from the government or its silence. It reiterated its resolve to curb the unabated inflow of 'outsiders' and to oppose the state government's move.

The sustained campaign saw Manipur valley crippled by strikes and shutdowns. The state government was pushed to the brink after a protesting student, Sapam Robinhood, died after a tear gas shell reportedly hit him during a rally in Imphal. The government was finally forced to withdraw the Bill. It then hurriedly constituted a panel to draft a new Bill, promising to incorporate, more or less, all the demands put forth by the JCILPS.

Five Key Demands

The drafting panel later stated its intention to incorporate all the five demands set by the JCILPS in an attempt to end a stalemate. The key demands were: (i) issuing passes to migrant workers arriving from outside the state at various entry points; (ii) making 1951 the cut-off base-year for implementation of the Bill; (iii) denying land ownership rights to migrants who entered Manipur after 1951; (iv) strengthening the Labour Department for the registration and regulation of inter-state migrant labourers; and (v) detection and deportation of illegal immigrants.

Although observers welcomed the government's willingness to incorporate the essential components of the JCILPS's demands, they see it as too late and too little. Certain quarters also view the government's intention with suspicion. This trust deficit was triggered primarily by the manner in which the government had disregarded the wisdom of those spearheading the movement to protect the rights of indigenous communities. By insisting on drafting a Bill that was within the ambit of the constitution, the state government was seen to be anxious not to displease New Delhi.

The Three Bills

Then, another round of violence came with the passing of three Bills: (i) The Protection of Manipur Peoples (PMP) Bill, 2015; (ii) The Manipur Land Revenues and Land Reforms (MLR&LR) (7th Amendment) Bill, 2015; and (iii) The Manipur Shops and Establishment (MS&E) (2nd Amendment) Bill, 2015 on August 31, 2015. These Bills were passed in the state assembly without any objections from the elected representatives on the last day of the emergency sitting of the 11th Session (Part-III) of the 10th Manipur legislative assembly.[5] The Bills were introduced and passed after the government supposedly incorporated the key demands of the JCILPS and after signing an agreement on August 25.

The Protection of Manipur Peoples (PMP) Bill, 2015

The highlights of the PMP Bill, 2015 included the establishment of a Directorate of Registration of non-Manipur persons and tenants where "the Director (rank of Class-I officer of the state government) will supervise the registration and issue of passes to the non-Manipur individuals and receipts to the owners hosting the tenants. The Director will have other administrative powers and functions as prescribed.

Issue of Pass: The registration authority will issue a pass to a non-Manipur person specifying his place of origin and the period of stay which will not be more than six months from the date of issue the period of stay may be extended from time to time by the Director.

Compulsory registration of non-Manipur persons and tenants: Every land and house owner who lets out accommodation to a non-Manipur person will have to maintain a register and enter the name and particulars of every non-Manipur persons as a tenant. The particulars of such entries are to be submitted by the owner to the Director every fortnight.

Offence and Penalty: Any owner who fails to furnish the names and particulars of the tenants to the Director within the period specified will be punishable with a fine up to a minimum of Rs. 2,000 but not exceeding Rs. 5,000.

Persons to be exempted: Those exempted from the purview of the Bill include persons employed with the Union Government, the state government, public undertaking and persons employed by a local authority or a body established by law with the approval of the state government, high dignitaries, students of educational institutions situated in the state or such other persons as may be determined by the state government from time to time" (*see* Hueiyen Lanpao, 2015).

Manipur Land Revenues and Land Reforms (Seventh Amendment) Bill, 2015 (MLR&LR)

MLR&LR's section 14-A says that "non-Manipur persons, firms, institutions or any other similar entities who intend to purchase any land in Manipur shall submit an application to the Deputy Commissioner of the district concerned where the land to be purchased is situated for obtaining the prior approval of the state government before such purchase is made by him" (*see* Hueiyen Lanpao, 2015).

Section 14B states that "allotment of land to non-Manipur persons, firms, institutions or any other similar entities would be made by the government after obtaining prior approval of the state cabinet" (*see* Hueiyen Lanpao, 2015).

Manipur Shops and Establishment (Second Amendment) Bill, 2015

Some highlights of the MS&E are as follows: Amendment of section 2 Clause (6) says that 'who is registered with, and issued a valid identity card by the registering officer' shall be inserted in between the words 'a person' and 'wholly' and that 'every employer shall register the names and particulars of employees employed within a week of employment with the Registering Officer'. The identity card issued under sub-section (2), shall be valid for a period of one year from the date of registration of the employee by the registering officer and shall be renewable for every one year, said the bill (*see* Hueiyen Lanpao, 2015).

After the three Bills were passed, there were violent protests in the hill areas particularly in Churachandpur district that led to the death of nine persons. Many hill-based organisations have called the three bills 'anti-tribal' and argued that these Bills violated the provision of Article 371(C) and the Manipur State Hill People Regulation, 1947. A state government press release published on September 2, 2015 clarified that the three Bills do not infringe on the existing rights of the tribal communities and also do not impinges on the provision of Article 371(C) and the subsequent Presidential Order of 1972 which provides for the Scheduled Areas and matters as also the Manipur State Hill People Regulation, 1947. It also clarified that the amendment of The Manipur Land Revenue and Land Reforms Act (MLR&LR) passed in the assembly does not extend to the hill areas, and in no way, it will affect or alter the present status of the tribal land. There seems to be 'misinterpretation and misunderstanding of the provisions of the Bills' leading to the tragic incidents causing tremendous losses including human lives, the release said while appealing all sections of the society to maintain peace and calm in Manipur.[6]

The All Tribal Students' Union, Manipur (ATSUM) had accused the state government of drafting and passing the Bill as per the 'wish and whims' of the JCILPS without any representation from the tribal representatives in the legislative assembly. To further cement their argument, the student group stated that the Manipur Rajas never ruled the hill tribes and it was the British who brought the hill areas within the fold of Manipur and engaged with them indirectly through the British Political Agent. The tribal student body said that even after Manipur was annexed by British in 1891, the hill areas were kept under the President of the Durbar and argued that the demands for the inner line permit were designed 'with an intention to empower the dominant community against the interest of the minority tribal population'.

The student group also alleged that legislative assembly committed 'grave constitutional blunder intentionally' as it did not follow the mandatory Rules of Procedures and Conduct of Business under Section 4, Clause 1 and 2 of the legislative assembly envisaged under Article 371(C). Even as the government responded by pointing out that the three Bills were 'money bills under 371C (2)', the student group objected to Section 2 of the Protection of Manipur People's Bill, 2015 which said that the regulation shall be extended to the whole of Manipur and demanded that the same should be extended only to the valley districts only.

However, the primary bone of contention put forth by the Zomi Council was about the definition of the 'Manipur People' in the Protection of Manipur Peoples (PMP) Bill, 2015.[7] The Zomi Council while asserting that the Bill was against the interest of the tribal people, termed the legislation as a 'hidden agenda' against the 'native tribal / hill populace' of Manipur. In a memorandum submitted to the Governor, the Zomi Council stated that 'the valley people want to grab the land of the tribals in the hill areas'. It pointed out that in the Clause 2 (b) of the MPB bill, the 'Manipur People' has been defined a 'persons' of Manipur whose names are on the National Register of Citizens, 1951, census report of 1951 and village directory of 1951 and their descendants who have 'contributed collective social, cultural and economic life of Manipur'.

The Zomi Council argued that this definition of 'Manipur People' would leave out 'many people' as, during the period mentioned in the Bill, the government 'machinery or governance had not reached every nook and corner' of Manipur especially the hill areas and most of the 'villages were not accessible at that time'. The Zomi Council further questioned why the Bill made the 'cut-off year' as 1951 and not 1971 or 1981 as Manipur attained statehood in 1972. The Zomi Council added if the definition is operationally applied, most of the natives of Manipur at the time when it attained statehood will not be considered 'Manipur People'. Based on this parameter, 80 per cent of the villages in the hill areas would be rendered 'unofficial and liable to be derecognised by the government', the Zomi Council noted.

While organisations and groups in both the hills and valley have locked horns over the passing of the Bills intended to protect the interests of the people collectively, the tension already sparked by mistrust and loss of confidence has been overwhelming. There are many other ways to understand the standoff as it stands now. One thing any perceptive observer would notice is the overlapping of identity politics with the rights discourse. What is even more interesting is that all the arguments citing historical commissions and omissions have centered on demand for protective rights. While doing so, both the opponents and supporters of the inner line permit as devised by the state government seem to have fallen trap to a self-imposed restriction and the overarching legal framework. Along the way, the finer details of separating the legal component from the political core have been blurred, rendering the current dispensation virtually helpless.

While one can see the potential difficulties inherent in contravening the constitution, very few have dared to seek and unravel the political component of the demands made so far. All the efforts made have been governed purely by the expediency of the legal framework. What the government failed to see is that all legal enactments around the world have been triggered by the need to consider the political core of any movement or situation. And it is this core that the ruling dispensation failed to consider.

Impasse Continues

Two of the Bills (The Manipur Land Revenue and Land Reforms (7th Amendment) Bill 2015 and The Manipur Shops and Establishments (2nd Amendment) Bill 2015) were withheld by the Union Government for 'consideration with experts'. This prompted the JCILPS to put pressure on the state government to pass a new Bill. The JCILPS leadership who had also learned from past mistakes began holding consultations with other communities in a move to seek consensus. The JCILPS and Kuki Students

Organisation had apparently agreed to launch a joint movement for the implementation of the inner line permit as they realised that the earlier Bills were rejected due to the lack of understanding among the different ethnic groups.

In one of the latest developments, on May 23, 2018, the state government constituted a committee to draft a new Bill. Subsequently, the Manipur People Bill, 2018 was introduced in the state assembly on August 20, 2018. This time there was no overt opposition from the people in the hill districts.

Notes

1. The paper is the updated version of the paper titled 'Inner Line Permit System: Manipur's Battle Within', published in *Eastern Quarterly*, 11(III & IV), Autumn & Winter 2015, 124–131.
2. JCILPS is made up of key organisations and was established in 2012. It is the committee formed to coordinate and spearhead the movement for the demand of Inner Line Permit System in Manipur.
3. Arambam Noni and Naorem Kishorchand. 2015. 'Living with an indecent State', *e-pao.net*, July 29.
4. Read: The Bengal Eastern Frontier Regulation, 1873.
5. '3 Bills for protection of Indigenous people passed', *Hueiyen Lanpao* (English Edition), September 1, 2015,
6. '3 Bills do not infringe on the existing rights of tribal communities in Manipur: Govt', *Hueiyen Lanpao*, September 2, 2015.
7. 'Zomi Council urges Guv to withdraw bills', *The Sangai Express*, September 1, 2015.

References

Arun, M.C. 2001. 'Students Politics in Manipuri Society', in Thomas, C. Joshua, et al, *Constraints in Development of Manipur*. New Delhi: Regency Publications, 39-56.

Chishti, SMAW. 2005. *Political Development in Manipur 1919-1949*. Delhi: Kalpaz Publications.

Hueiyen Lanpao. 2015. 'Bills for protection of Indigenous people introduced', *Hueiyen Lanpao*, August 28.

JCILPS. 2012. 'Why does Manipur require Inner Line Permit System?' *The Sangai Express*, October 29.

Tarapot, Phanjoubam. 2003, *Bleeding Manipur*. New Delhi: Har-Anand Publications.

Contributors

Anamika Deb Roy is Assistant Professor at the Centre for North East Studies and Policy Research, Jamia Millia Islamia, New Delhi. Her research interests include gender roles, folkloristic, and emerging literary cultures from Northeast India.

Angom Sangeeta is Assistant Professor at the National Institute of Educational Planning and Administration, New Delhi. Her research areas are governance, privatisation, and academic reforms.

Arobindo Mahato is Coordinator of the Department of Rural Studies, Tripura University. Arobindo research areas include rural sociology, social policy and quantitative social research. Specialised in livelihood, migration, border-related issues, environment-friendly technology etc.

Dolly Limbu presently teaches at the Department of English, D.M. College of Arts, Dhanamanjuri University, Imphal. Her areas of interests include popular culture, identity and cinema studies. Her current research work focuses on understanding the trope of Nepali identity in an ethnically and culturally divergent state of Manipur. She has formerly taught at Jamia Millia Islamia and colleges affiliated to Delhi University.

Dhiren A. Sadokpam is an independent researcher and journalist based in Manipur. Sadokpam has co-edited 'Northeast India: A Reader' 2018, published by Routledge UK and India. He has worked both in print and electronic media since 1996 and is currently engaged with independent works on media, culture and the political economy of Northeast India.

Immanuel Zarzosang Varte is Assistant Professor (contract), Department of Tribal Studies, Indira Gandhi National Tribal University-Regional Campus Manipur. His area of expertise and interest includes development, culture, peace and conflict studies.

Huidrom Renuka is a Ph.D student at the Special Centre for the Study of North East India, Jawaharlal Nehru University, New Delhi. She is working on 'Dam and Development: A Study of Socio-Economic and Political Dynamics in Mapithel, Manipur.' Her research interest includes culture, development, displacement, livelihood and environmental ecology.

K. N. Tennyson is Assistant Professor at the Afghanistan Studies Programme, MMAJ Academy of International Studies, Jamia Millia Islamia, New Delhi. He is an alumnus of the School of International Studies, Jawaharlal Nehru University, New Delhi. He was associated with the Centre for Air Power Studies, New Delhi. His research interest includes Afghanistan, India's Foreign Policy, Northeast India politics and South Asian security issues.

M. Amarjeet Singh is Professor at the Centre for North East Studies and Policy Research, Jamia Millia Islamia (A Central University), New Delhi, where he teaches courses in social conflict and identity politics; and society and politics. His research focuses on conflict studies, identity politics and migration studies.

M. Stelin Singh is Assistant Professor at Rajiv Gandhi University, Itanagar. His area of specialisation is molecular reproduction.

Mrinal Kanti Deb is Doctoral Scholar at the Department of Rural Studies, Tripura University. He is pursuing Ph.D on 'Migration from Bangladesh and its Impact on Rural Livelihood in Northeast India'. Mrinal's research interests include labour migration, rural livelihood and tribal development.

Ningthoujam Rameshchandra is an ICSSR Post-Doctoral Research Fellow at the Department of Economics, Sikkim University. His research interest areas among others are migration, conflict, and nationalism.

Rita Chakma is a Ph.D student at the Department of Sociology, Tripura University working on religious life of the Chakmas: A sociological analysis of transformative streams. She is at present working for government media under the Government of Tripura.

Sneha Mishra is a Ph.D scholar at the Department of Economics, Sikkim University. She is pursuing Ph.D on 'Livelihood sustainability of migrant labourers from Bihar in Northeast India: A comparative study of Assam and Sikkim.' Sneha's research interests include casual labour migration, livelihood sustainability and migration.

Index